More
Prayers
that Prevail

More Prayers that Prevail

–Volume 2–
of
The Believer's
Manual
of Prayers

By
Clift Richards & Lloyd Hildebrand

VICTORY HOUSE PUBLISHERS
Tulsa, Oklahoma

MORE PRAYERS THAT PREVAIL
Copyright © 1995 by K & C International, Inc.
ISBN 0-932081-46-0

Published by Victory House, Inc.
P.O. Box 700238
Tulsa, Oklahoma 74170
(918) 747-5009

Contents

Prayer Changes Everything!

The Serenity Prayer, first penned by Reinhold Neibuhr, a German theologian, gives us a biblical perspective concerning prayer and living. Its words are familiar to many of us:

God, grant me the serenity to accept the things I cannot change; courage, to change the things I can; and wisdom to know the difference.

Two things we cannot change are the past and other people. It is our attitudes toward people and the circumstances of our lives that we can change, however, and prayer has the dynamic power to effect these essential changes in our lives. As Soren Kierkegaard, a Danish philosopher and theologian, affirmed, "Prayer does not change God; it changes the one who prays." As prayer changes the attitudes of your heart, the circumstances of your life will frequently fall into place. This is how God chooses to operate, even though it defies all attempts at logical explanation.

The purpose of this chapter, therefore, is to show how prayer has provided individual believers with courage to change the things they can, and wisdom to discern between things they can and cannot change. In each of the examples we present you will notice how prayer changes the individual as well as his or her circumstances.

Prayer in the Old Testament

The Hebrew people recognized God as "O you who hear prayer" (Ps. 65:2, NIV). Often, the Israelites prayed to God in conversational form. This is typified in the Garden of Eden, where Adam and Eve "...heard the sound of the Lord God walking in the garden in the cool of the day,...Then the Lord God called to Adam and said to him, 'Where are you?' So he said, 'I heard Your voice in the garden, and I was afraid...'" (Gen. 3:8-10, NKJV).

Often, in those early days, people would do something tangible to symbolize their encounters with God. Some would erect shrines, others would give immediate obedience to God's commands, and some, such as Job, would question the meaning God was trying to convey.

Prayer — A Dialogue With God

It is important to recognize that prayer to these early believers was a dialogue (a two-way conversation) with God, not a monologue (a long speech that monopolizes a conversation).

To them, prayer was a conversation with God, and it should be the same for every believer today. We believe that God is there, that He hears us, and that He responds to our prayers. This is a truth that Zacharias needed to be assured of, and so the angel came to him with this exciting message: "Do not be afraid, Zacharias; for your prayer is heard" (Luke 1:13, NKJV). This is a message of comfort to each praying believer today as well.

> *But without faith it is impossible to please*
> *Him; for he who comes to God must believe that*
> *He is, and that He is a rewarder of those who*
> *diligently seek Him.*
>
> (Heb. 11:6, NKJV)

The Cloud of Witnesses

The writer of the Book of Hebrews shows us how the Old Testament patriarchs of faith responded to God in prayer. (See Heb. 11.) Noah, for example, was warned by God about the Flood, and he responded with faith and obedience. As a result, both the attitudes of his heart and the circumstances of his life, and the lives of members of his family, were transformed.

Abraham, likewise, heard God's voice directing him to leave Ur of the Chaldees in order to enter a land he did not know. "By faith he sojourned in the land of promise, as in a strange country, dwelling in tabernacles with Isaac and Jacob, the heirs with him of the same promise" (Heb. 11:8-9).

The Book of Hebrews reveals how prayer changed the lives and circumstances of Joseph, Sarah, Jacob, Moses, Joshua, Samuel, David, and many others. These prayer warriors left an eternal example for all of us to follow; it is a rich and precious inheritance that has been bestowed upon us by men and women of prayer. What's more, these same believers continue to encourage us, as the writer of Hebrews declares, "Therefore, since we are surrounded by such a great cloud of witnesses [those people of faith who have gone before us], let us throw off everything that hinders and the sin that so easily entangles, and let us run with perseverance the race marked out for us. Let us fix our eyes on Jesus, the author and perfecter of our faith...." (Heb. 12:1-2, NIV).

As the early believers, who are now the "cloud of witnesses" that is cheering us on, reflected on God's mercies in their lives, they were impelled to pray and worship. They adored their heavenly Father, loved Him, and surrendered their lives into His care. In return, He gave them many blessings and promises.

This book takes those promises seriously. We believe the promises of God that have been revealed in the holy Scriptures, and we have formed the prayers within this book accordingly. As you meditate upon God's Word, as it is found in the topical prayers, your faith will be strengthened, and you will be enabled to reach out and appropriate the truthful promises of God in your own life. This is our prayer for you.

Face to Face With God

Continuing our look at prayer in the Old Testament, we see God speaking to Moses "...face to face, as a man speaks to his friend" (Exod. 33:11, NKJV). This is the relationship God wants to have with us today. As Jesus said, "You are My friends if you do whatever I command you" (John 15:14, NKJV). He also said, "My sheep hear my voice, and I know them, and they follow me" (John 10:27). Yes, it is possible to hear the voice of God when we pray.

Indeed, this should be a major goal of our praying. Let us focus on the development of profound personal intimacy with God through prayer. The ancient prophet Isaiah shows us what can happen when we make this a priority in our praying: "Your ears shall hear a word behind you, saying, 'This is the way, walk in it,' Whenever you turn to the right hand Or whenever you turn to the left" (Isa. 30:21, NKJV).

God, our Father, wants an intimate, personal relationship with all His children, and as you "Draw nigh to God,...he will draw nigh to you" (James 4:8). As you read *More Prayers That Prevail*, it is our prayer that you will develop that deeply personal intimacy with God that will enable all your prayers to become a dialogue with the One who wants so much to have a personal relationship with you, His special child. Everything in your life will change as a result of that wonderful intimacy that is cultivated and fostered through prayer.

One Thing Is Needed

When Jesus, our Lord and Savior, visited in the home of the two sisters, Mary and Martha, he rebuked Martha for her impatience that stemmed from a deep-seated performance orientation which means that she wanted to please Jesus by way of her works. Perhaps she felt that He would not accept her if she were not perfect in every respect. Mary, on the other hand, wanted to get to know the Master, and He complimented her: "But one thing is needed, and Mary has chosen that good part, which will not be taken away from her" (Luke 10:42, NKJV). "That good part" is prayer and worship — two vital components in our relationship with the Lord. The gospel chorus describes it well: "I have something that the world can't give, and the world can't take it away." That special "something" is an intimate, abiding personal relationship with Jesus and our Father in heaven.

The saints and patriarchs of the Old Testament knew the meaning of this concept from personal experience. All of them — the prophets, the Psalmist, the kings, and patriarchs — knew the power of prayer. Their prayers prevailed because they believed God. They took Him at His Word. Sarah's prayers prevailed, for example, because she knew and trusted the Lord. King David's prayers, as recorded in the Book of Psalms, prevailed because he had made sure to build a personal, honest relationship with the Lord, his Shepherd. For Hosea, prayer had to be a matter of the heart, as we see in the following verse: "They did not cry out to Me with their heart" (Hos. 7:14, NKJV). God wants us to cry to Him with our hearts, our souls, our minds, and all our strength. He yearns for a close relationship with all His people, and He wants His people to make this their hearts' desire as well.

The prophet Jeremiah often prays in the form of a personal meditation. Similarly, the prayers that form the body of this book are styled to be meditational in format. By meditating upon God's Word as you pray, counting your blessings instead of your losses, you will find a whole new perspective that will enable you to rise above any negative circumstances of your life and transcend your problems. Notice how the prophet Jeremiah prays, "O Lord, I know the way of man is not in himself; It is not in man who walks to direct his own steps. O Lord, correct me, but with justice; Not in Your anger, lest You bring me to nothing" (Jer. 10:23-24, NKJV). As Jeremiah meditates upon the human condition in his prayer, he recognizes his personal need for God's intervention in his life. By doing so, he is cultivating an honest, trusting relationship with his Father.

A Prayerful Heart

In learning to pray *More Prayers That Prevail*, we should keep Jeremiah's example in our minds and hearts. The attitude of his prayerful heart is worthy of emulation. Jeremiah was actually seeking that vital component of our faith that leads to fruitfulness in all our endeavors, including prayer. John the Baptist echoed this approach when he pointed out, "He must increase, but I must decrease" (John 3:30). Jesus reminded us of this truth when He said, "Without Me you can do nothing" (John 15:5, NKJV). This is the heart-attitude that leads us to pray with power, and it leads to victorious living such as that described by the Apostle Paul: "I can do all things through Christ who strengthens me" (Phil. 4:13, NKJV). Yes, without Jesus we can do nothing, but through Him we can do all things!

The Old Testament gives us several examples of personal prayer. The practice of personal prayer is revealed most vividly in the Book of Psalms — a book of meditations, prayers, and praise in the form of songs and poetry. They incorporate all the effective aspects of prevailing prayer — adoration, thanksgiving, praise, trust, intercession, confession, and petition. They are heart-felt prayers that reveal deep human emotions and struggles that most of us can identify with.

The foundation for effective prayer is permanently laid in the Old Testament. Our prayer should be like the

Psalmist's: "O Lord, hear my voice. Let your ears be attentive to my cry for mercy....I wait for the Lord, my soul waits, and in his word I put my hope. My soul waits for the Lord more than watchmen wait for the morning" (Ps. 130:2, 5-6, NIV).

Prayer in the New Testament

Jesus is, for all time, the foremost example of a true prayer warrior and intercessor. He spent a great deal of time in prayer. This, more than anything else, provided Him with the energy He needed to fulfill His ministry on earth. In heaven, where He now resides, Jesus "...always lives to make intercession" (Heb. 7:25, NKJV) for us. His succinct, yet comprehensive model prayer (the Lord's Prayer) provides us with a perfect outline for us to use in the development of our prayer life. (See our first book, *Prayers That Prevail*, for additional teaching on this vital subject.)

Our Lord and Master teaches us that anxiety prevents us from prevailing in prayer. Conversely, that anxiety is evaporated by earnest prayer. He shows us that we must spend much time in secret prayer, because "...your Father who sees in secret will reward you openly" (Matt. 6:18, NKJV). He commands us to: "Ask and it will be given to you; seek and you will find; knock and the door will be opened to you. For everyone who asks receives; he who seeks finds; and to him who knocks, the door will be opened" (Matt. 7:7-8, NIV).

Our Lord Jesus connected fasting with prayer. Like Moses, He fasted for forty days and nights when He was being tested in the wilderness. Through prayer and fasting,

Jesus was able to defeat Satan by simply speaking the Word of God. In the same way, we will be able to defeat the enemy. Concerning spiritual warfare, Jesus once pointed out to His disciples, "This kind [of demonic spirit] can come forth by nothing, but by prayer and fasting" (Mark 9:29). Through fasting, a believer's heart is able to focus more clearly on spiritual truths, instead of physical needs, as he or she prays.

Earnest Intercession

Jesus, as we have already pointed out, is the ultimate Intercessor. He is our High Priest who is "...touched with the feeling of our infirmities" (Heb. 4:15). The Apostle Paul was also a great intercessor. Through the prayerful examples of Jesus and Paul the early church realized the importance of prayer. Paul wrote, "I exhort therefore, that, first of all, supplications, prayers, intercessions, and giving of thanks, be made for all men...." (1 Tim. 2:1). The early believers realized that spiritually vital prayer was obligatory if they were to live spiritually prevailing lives.

James revealed a practical application of intercessory prayer in his epistle: "Is any one of you sick? He should call the elders of the church to pray over him and anoint him with oil in the name of the Lord. And the prayer offered in faith will make the sick person well; the Lord will raise him up. If he has sinned, he will be forgiven" (James 5:14-16, NIV). James, like Jesus, Paul, and the other apostles, fully recognized the essential aspect of faith in all our praying.

God initiates our desire to pray. It is a drawing of His Spirit to ours, seeking communion with those He has created to enjoy fellowship with Him. God offers restoration to anyone who comes to Him. The Spirit of God prompts us to pray so that we can enter into all that God has graciously prepared for those who love Him. The Spirit intercedes for us with "groanings which cannot be uttered" (Rom. 8:26). When we do not know what to pray for, or how to pray, the Holy Spirit leads us and guides us into all truth.

> *Now He who searches the hearts knows what the mind of the Spirit is, because He makes intercession for the saints according to the will of God. And we know that all things work together for good to those who love God, to those who are the called according to His purpose.* (Rom. 8:27-28, NKJV)

Through prayer, as Paul points out, we discover what our true needs are. God already knows what we need, as Jesus said in the Gospel According to Matthew: "...your Father knows what you need before you ask him" (Matt. 6:8, NIV). Prayer conforms our desires to those the Father has for us, and it leads us to delight in His will at all times, even when conditions around us are not the greatest. Paul wrote, "Be anxious for nothing, but in everything by prayer and supplication, with thanksgiving, let your requests be made known to God; and the peace of God, which surpasses all understanding, will guard your hearts and minds through Christ Jesus" (Phil. 4:6-7, NKJV). What more could anyone want in this life? ✓

Prayer in Church History

The greatest sustaining factor in the lives of Christians throughout the centuries has been prayer. It has enabled countless martyrs to face burning at the stake, the "hot seat" of ancient Rome, decapitation, imprisonment, mockery, persecution, misunderstanding, torture, and injustice. Most of the martyrs turned to God in audible prayers of trust as they went to their executions. Stephen, the first Christian martyr, followed in the footsteps of Jesus by forgiving his enemies. (See Acts 7.) This brave young man called upon God, saying, "'Lord Jesus, receive my spirit.' Then he knelt down and cried out with a loud voice, 'Lord, do not charge them with this sin.' And when he had said this, he fell asleep" (Acts 7:59-60, NKJV).

The last words of many Christians have been prayers. John Huss, for example, faced his martyrdom with this prayer: "Jesus Christ, the Son of the living God, have mercy upon me." Soon thereafter the flames consumed him. John Wycliffe, the famous Bible translator, uttered the words of the Bible as a prayer just before his death. He prayed a Psalm: "I shall not die, but live, and declare the works of the Lord" (Ps. 118:17).

It was prayer that fortified our Lord and Savior, Jesus Christ, on the night before His crucifixion: "Father, if it is Your will, take this cup away from Me; nevertheless not My will, but Yours be done" (Luke 22:42, NKJV). Immediately thereafter, an angel of God appeared to Him and strengthened Him. The prayers of Jesus, and the prayers of the martyrs, were truly *Prayers That Prevail* in that their prayers enabled them to make the ultimate sacrifice for God.

Jesus admonishes us to "Watch therefore, and pray always that you may be counted worthy to escape all these things that will come to pass, and to stand before the Son of Man" (Luke 21:36, NKJV). Prayer will always enable believers to prevail without regard to the circumstances of life.

Prayer Warriors

David Brainerd, a Presbyterian missionary to the Native Americans, devised a beautiful metaphor for the life of prayer and the changes it brings to the human spirit: "When the dragon-fly rends his husk and harnesses himself in a clean plate of sapphire mail, his is a pilgrimage of one or two sunny days over the fields and pastures wet with dew, yet nothing can exceed the marvelous beauty in which he is decked. No flowers on earth have a richer blue than the pure color of his cuirass. So is it in the high spiritual sphere. The most complete spiritual loveliness may be obtained in the shortest time, and the stripling may die a hundred years old, in character and in grace." (From *The History of David Brainerd.*)

As E.M. Bounds points out, "God has not confined himself to Old and New Testament times in employing praying men as His agents in furthering His cause on earth, and He has placed himself under obligation to answer their prayers just as much as He did the saints of old." (From *The Weapon of Prayer* by E.M. Bounds.)

George Mueller of Bristol, England, was an example of this truth. He truly believed the words of Jesus: "For with God nothing shall be impossible" (Luke 1:37). Mueller's work with orphans proved this scriptural fact.

Mueller covenanted with his heavenly Father that he would never express his needs, and the needs of his orphans, to anyone but God himself. This he faithfully did in daily prayer. As a result, the needs of the orphans were frequently met by miraculous means. As a case in point, there was a time when the cupboards of the orphanage were completely bare. Fully believing that God would supply all their needs, according to His promise, Mueller directed the boys to set the table for dinner even though he had nothing to serve them. They obeyed, and after the table was set, they all joined in prayer. As they were praying, a knock could be heard at the door. It was a railman from a freight train that was transporting food from one city to another. The train had derailed while they were praying, and since the food was perishable, the man offered the entire trainload of food, including meats and vegetables to George Mueller and his orphans! Mueller had taken his stand on God's promise: "But my God shall supply all your need according to his riches in glory by Christ Jesus" (Phil. 4:15).

Claimed a miracle.

God moves in mysterious ways in response to the prevailing prayers of believers. Jesus said, "Therefore do not worry, saying, 'What shall we eat?' or 'What shall we drink?' or, 'What shall we wear?'...For your heavenly Father knows that you need all these things. But seek first the kingdom of God and His righteousness, and all these things shall be added to you" (Matt. 6:31-33, NKJV). From personal experience, George Mueller and his orphans learned that God's Word can be trusted completely and implicitly. God cannot fail.

Rees Howells, a great intercessor of the twentieth century, prayed for God's intervention to avert further bloodshed during World War II. God heard his prayers, and He graciously intervened.

Missionaries the world over know and treasure the value of prayer. Henry Martyn was a missionary to India in the early part of the nineteenth century. He wrote, "What a knowledge of man and acquaintance with the Scriptures, and what communion with God and study of my own heart ought to prepare me for the awful work of a messenger from God on business of the soul."

Every effective minister and missionary knows the truth of Martyn's words. To be effective in ministry, an individual must give himself to prayer, as the first-century apostles did so faithfully. Prayer is the source of power to minister, and when prayer is combined with the power of God's Word, as the topical prayers of this book are, exciting results are to be expected, because God always confirms His Word to the hearts of believers.

Henry Martyn's ministry was fruitful in direct proportion to the time he spent in prayer. One observer of his life wrote, "By daily weighing the Scriptures, with prayer, he waxed riper and riper in his ministry. Prayer and the holy Scriptures were those wells of salvation out of which he drew daily the living water for his thirsty immortal soul. Truly may it be said of him, he prayed always with all prayer and supplication, in the Spirit, and watched thereunto with all perseverance." The result of Martyn's faithful (and faith-filled) life of prayer was the conversion of hundreds of Hindus to the cause of Christ.

Jonathan Edwards, an important leader in America's Great Awakening, was a man of prayer. (See *Prayers That*

Prevail for Your Children for additional insights into the effects of prayer in the life of Edwards and his family.) Edwards wrote in his diary, "Once as I rode out in the woods for my health, having alighted from my horse in a retired place, as my manner has been to walk for divine contemplation and prayer, I had a view, that for me was extraordinary, of the glory of the Son of God as Mediator between God and man, and of His wonderful, great, full, pure, and sweet grace and love, and His meek and gentle condescension. This grace that seemed so calm and sweet, appeared also great above the heavens. The person of Christ appeared ineffably excellent with an excellency yet enough to swallow up all thought and conception, which continued, as near as I can judge, about an hour. It kept me the greater part of the time in a flood of tears and weeping aloud. I felt an ardency of soul to be, what I know not otherwise how to express, emptied and annihilated, to lie in the dust; to be full of Christ alone, to love Him with my whole heart." Edwards's great personal awakening through prayer would soon be experienced by thousands of others. It led this man of God to intercede for the nation, and a heaven-borne revival swept our land. The same could happen today, and this should be an important focus of all our prayers.

Charles G. Finney, another famous revivalist, wrote, "When God has specially promised the thing, we are bound to believe we shall receive it when we pray for it. You have no right to put in an 'if,' and say, 'Lord, if it be thy will, give me thy Holy Spirit.' This is to insult God. To put an 'if' in God's promise when God has put none there, is tantamount to charging God with being insincere. It is like saying, 'O God, if thou are in earnest in making these promises, grant us the blessing we pray for."

These scriptural thoughts are in our minds as we write this book, and we trust that they will remain in your heart as you pray. Truly, they are keys to *Prayers That Prevail.*

Adoniram Judson, a nineteenth-century missionary to Burma, believed in prevailing prayer. He wrote, "'Nothing is impossible,' said one of the seven sages of Greece, 'to industry.' Let us change the word 'industry' to 'persevering prayer,' and the motto will be more Christian and more worthy of universal adoption. God loves importunate prayer so much that He will not give us much blessing without it. God says, 'Behold I will do a new thing; now it shall spring forth; shall ye not know it? I will even make a way in the wilderness and rivers in the desert. This people have I formed for myself; they shall shew forth my praise.'" It is the people who learn to pray in a prevailing fashion who will be enabled, through prayer, to show forth God's praise.

Martin Luther, the father of the Protestant Reformation, was a man of prayer. He prayed for his church, his friends, his nation, and his own needs. Through diligent prayer and study, he discovered the liberating truth that "the just shall live by faith." When Luther was accused of heresy, he turned to God in prayer. The Lord delivered him, gave him wisdom, and imparted to His servant a courage that enabled him to remain steadfast and true in the face of much opposition. On his death-bed, Luther prayed, "My heavenly Father, eternal and merciful God, you have mani-fested unto me your dear son, our Lord Jesus Christ. I have taught Him, I have known Him; I love Him as my life, my

health, and my redemption. Whom the wicked have persecuted, maligned, and with injury afflicted. Draw my soul
to thee." He then commended his spirit to God, and quoted
a Scripture:

> *For God so loved the world, that he gave his*
> *only begotten Son, that whosoever believeth in*
> *him should not perish, but have everlasting life.*
> *(John 3:16)*

Charles Spurgeon, like Luther, knew his God was a
prayer-answering Father. He wrote this prayer: "Lord
Jesus, cause me to know in my daily experience the glory
and sweetness of thy name, and then teach me how to use
it in my prayer, so that I may be even like Israel, a prince
prevailing with God. Thy name is my passport, and
secures me access; thy name is my plea, and secures me
answer; thy name is my honor and secures me glory.
Blessed Name, thou art honey in my mouth, music in my
ear, heaven in my heart, and all in all to all my being." God
heard and answered Spurgeon's prayer by allowing His
servant to become like Israel, an evangelist who prevailed
through prayer, ushering thousands into the Kingdom of
God.

Prayer continues to be a powerful tool in evangelism
and revival. Before every Billy Graham crusade, for
example, hundreds of believers beseech God to bring
revival to their cities. God hears and answers the prayers
of His people. Indeed, every revival in church history was
birthed in believing prayer.

Dr. A.J. Gordon points to the importance of prayer in
evangelism: "The deepest need of the Church today is not

for any material or external thing, but the deepest need is spiritual. Prayerless work will never bring in the kingdom. We neglect to pray in the prescribed way. We seldom enter the closet and shut the door for a season of prayer. Kingdom interests are pressing on us thick and fast and we must pray. Prayerless giving will never evangelize the world."

The deepest need of our time remains within the spiritual realm. It will be realized and actualized through prevailing prayer. Let us keep in mind the following exhortation:

> *If my people, which are called by my name,*
> *shall humble themselves, and pray, and seek my*
> *face, and turn from their wicked ways; then will*
> *I hear from heaven, and will forgive their sin,*
> *and will heal their land. (2 Chron. 7:14)*

As we have noted, the effects of prayer in our lives and circumstances are wider than the horizons of earth, deeper than the oceans, and higher than the mountains. Within the individual, those effects include a deep sense of peace and well-being. Beyond these important elements, the pray-er experiences an abiding sense of God's presence. The person who prays is not only aware of God's presence, but frequently he or she senses that God is acknowledging his or her presence as well. In one recent study regarding prayer, seventy-two percent of those who were surveyed reported that they had received definite answers to specific prayer requests. Spiritual insights and revelations are received during times of prayer as well, and guidance from God is imparted to those who wait for His leading. Healings are often experienced as a result of prayer — healings of physical ailments as well as inner hurts of the heart and soul.

Robert W. Faid was an agnostic scientist who benefited from the prayers of his wife and other believers when he developed terminal cancer. As a result of their prevailing prayers, he was healed of cancer, and more importantly, he became a true believer in Jesus Christ and the power of prayer.

Through prayer, countless individuals have learned to forgive those who have hurt them. Corrie ten Boom was a lady who learned to forgive others through prayer. Her story is told in the book, *The Hiding Place*, an inspiring story of her family's struggles during the German holocaust. Corrie lost her father and her sister, Betsy, in the Nazi concentration camps. After the war, she was speaking in a German church, and she noticed one of the cruel camp guards sitting in the congregation. Fear and hatred gripped her heart as she realized that she might have to shake hands with this man after the service. It was prayer that enabled her to prevail by forgiving the man. At first, her feelings went against her being able to forgive him, but she set her will to obey the Lord who told her that she must forgive. Later, Corrie reported that she was able to look the former guard directly in the eyes and to lift her hand to take his. As she did so, the love of God coursed through her being, down her arm, into her hand, and presumably into the hand of the ex-Nazi. The power of her true Christian witness must have shaken the man immeasurably.✔

Those who prevail in prayer know the truth of the Psalmist's words: "Blessed are the people who know the joyful sound! They walk, O Lord, in the light of Your countenance. In Your name they rejoice all day long, And in Your righteousness shall they are exalted. For You are the glory of their strength, And in Your favor our horn is exalted" (Ps. 89:15-16, NKJV).

One modern businessman talks about his prayer experience this way, "I try to settle my spirit when I first come to prayer by sitting quietly with my eyes closed and letting go of my thoughts one by one as they arise. Usually, sooner or later, I feel empty and full at the same time. Empty of the business that usually fills my life, but full of a tranquil presence I can't really describe. Once this happens I am oblivious to my surroundings, indifferent to time and place. I seem to be filled with a transparent light that leaves me as content as a baby who has just been fed." This testimony reflects the power of prayer to change the attitudes of the human heart.

Yes, prayer changes things. In fact, prayer changes everything! As you focus on the promises of God that are presented in the prayers of this book, you will experience a variety of changes, both within and without. We know this to be true because countless readers of our first book, *Prayers That Prevail*, have reported that learning the style of Scripture-praying presented in our books has literally transformed their lives and the lives of others. One doctor, for example, had long been concerned about his son's underachievement in school. He reported that as they prayed "A Student's Prayer" (from *Prayers That Prevail*) together, dramatic changes occurred, including a strengthening of their relationship and greater academic success for the son.

A Russian Orthodox woman told us that she had received Jesus Christ as her personal Savior as she prayed the first prayer in *Prayers That Prevail*. Since that time, she has experienced great peace after a lifetime of almost-constant anxiety.

A pastor in a southern state was counseling with a young man who had a particular emotional issue in his life. The young man asked the pastor to teach him how to pray about the given concern. Not knowing exactly how to do so, the pastor glanced at his bookshelf and noticed a copy of *Prayers That Prevail* that was located there. His eyes were drawn to this book he had never read, and as he opened it, his eyes fell upon a topical prayer that addressed the young man's specific need. They prayed the prayer together, and the counselee experienced immediate deliverance from his problem.

The theme of *More Prayers That Prevail* is similar to the theme of our first book: *God answers the believing prayers of His people.* Andrew Murray puts it well, "The nearness of God gives rest and power in prayer. The nearness of God is given to him who makes it his first object. 'Draw nigh to God'; seek the nearness to Him, and He will give it; 'He will draw nigh to you.' Then it becomes easy to pray in faith."

Let this book be an open door to a new adventure in prayer for you as you reap all the fruits of faith that God has in store for you. He wants you to experience His presence and His peace for all eternity, and as you learn to pray in prevailing faith, He will lead you into new spiritual dimensions. He will set you free from those things that have always held you back. He will reveal His will to you.

Through prayer, you will find total and complete transformation in every area of your life. You will rejoice as you discover how prayer changes everything!

In conclusion, therefore, let's review some of the things that prevailing and believing prayer is capable of changing:

- The attitudes of our hearts.
- The circumstances of our lives.
- Our perspective.
- Our relationship with God.
- Our relationships with others.
- The course of our lives.
- Our thought processes.
- The focus of our minds.
- Unmet needs into answers.
- Our health.
- Our view of God, others, ourselves, and our circumstances.

Prayer transforms our lives by giving us peace instead of anxiety, hope instead of despair, faith instead of doubt, love instead of fear, trust instead of worry, and health instead of sickness. Prayer changes everything in our lives. As Alfred, Lord Tennyson pointed out, "More things are wrought by prayer than this world dreams of...."

Prayers in the Bible

The Bible records hundreds of prayers that serve as models for believers today. By examining some of these we are able to learn the principles of prevailing prayer, the dynamics of our relationship with God, the Father, and how God responds to heart-felt, believing prayer. This section of *More Prayers That Prevail* takes a look at many of these prayers so that we will be able to learn from the examples of Bible characters who believed in the power of prayer.

Abraham Prays for Sodom

The first book of the Bible, Genesis, like all other sixty-five books, reveals the importance of prayer in a believer's life. All the patriarchs were men of prayer, and they loved to pray. Prayer was always their first resort in dealing with the issues of their lives, their families, and their people. The founder of Judaism, Abraham, turned to prayer whenever he needed direction, hope, wisdom, and divine intervention.

The Bible tells us that Abraham (Abram) moved to the land of Canaan, and Lot, his nephew, pitched his tent toward Sodom. "But the men of Sodom were wicked and sinners before the Lord exceedingly" (Gen. 13:13). Sodom and

Gomorrah were twin cities that were filled with idolatry and
sinfulness of every description.

Abraham knew that God's wrath would fall upon
Sodom if the residents of the city failed to turn to their
Father in heaven. He became their intercessor; indeed, he
became a model intercessor for us today. He "stood yet
before the Lord," and he prayed, "Would You also destroy
the righteous with the wicked? Suppose there were fifty
righteous within the city; would you also destroy the place
and not spare it for the fifty righteous that were in it?"
(Gen. 18:23-24, NKJV).

The conversational style of prayer was employed by
Abraham as he endeavored to make intercession for the
people of Sodom. Prayer was a form of dialogue with God
to this man of faith, and the Lord responded, "If I find in
Sodom fifty righteous within the city, then I will spare all
the place for their sakes" (Gen. 18:26, NKJV). God heard
Abraham's cry, and He was moved with compassion by
Abraham's concern and the plight of the Sodomites.

The man of prayer approached the Lord once more; this
time he went before God's throne in abject humility: "Indeed
now, I who am but dust and ashes have taken it upon myself
to speak to the Lord: Suppose there were five less than the
fifty righteous; would You destroy all the city for lack of
five?" (Gen. 18:27-28, NKJV)

Through this conversation with God, Abraham was
seeking his Lord's will with regard to Sodom. He was
always careful to wait for answers from his heavenly
Father before proceeding with additional inquiries into His
will. The patriarch asked God if He would spare the city

for forty righteous people, then thirty righteous, then twenty, and ten. In each case, God told Abraham that He would not destroy the city if the particular numbers of righteous people cited by Abraham could be found within its gates.

It was a time of intense seeking, a time of learning about God and His ways, a time for hearing the voice of God. God was faithful to His servant and his family.

After this time of holy communion with God, Abraham found himself entertaining angels. In short order, those messengers of God realized that Sodom was beyond hope and they communicated to Lot that the Lord would destroy the city. This gave Lot, his wife, their sons, daughters, in-laws, and grandchildren the opportunity to flee before the destruction came.

Sodom Is Destroyed

"Then the Lord rained brimstone and fire on Sodom and Gomorrah, from the Lord out of the heavens. So He overthrew those cities, all the plain, all the inhabitants of the cities, and what grew on the ground" (Gen. 19:24-25, NKJV). That was the end of these two metropolitan centers of wickedness, and it was also the demise of Lot's wife who, as they were fleeing the city, looked back upon it wistfully. She was turned into a pillar of salt for doing so.

Abraham's prayer for Sodom was answered. God, in His justice and righteousness, could not permit such a wicked place, inhabited by so many wicked individuals, to continue to influence others. As a result of Abraham's prayer, however, the righteous members of his family were rescued from destruction.

What can we learn about effective praying from Abraham's example? First, true prayer is a two-way conversation with God. It involves our expression of our needs and wants and our waiting upon the Lord for an answer. God hears and answers prayer. He wants to have fellowship with His people; in fact, He loves times of communion with us. This is one of the primary purposes of prayer — to get to know God and His will better.

Abraham was persistent. He was not about to give up. He wanted to know God's will, and he persevered until he heard the voice of God, thereby receiving an answer to his prayer. In the process, Abraham was assured that God cared as much about the people of Sodom as he did. Through prayer, the father of monotheism (the worship of one God) was able to ascertain the will of God. In this way, he saw into the merciful heart of God, and learned about the justice of God as well. He also learned how to discern the voice of God through prayer.

Abraham approached God with humility. He was not arrogant, defiant, or demanding even though he was totally honest with God. In fact, he feared God in the sense that he feared His displeasure because he respected the heavenly Father so much. "The remarkable thing about fearing God," Oswald Chambers pointed out, "is that when you fear God you fear nothing else, whereas if you do not fear God you fear everything else" (From *The Highest Good* by Oswald Chambers). This fear of God, as demonstrated by Abraham, is best characterized as high respect, reverence, and honor for our Father in heaven. It leads to prevailing prayer and righteous living.

Moses' Prayer of Thanksgiving

When the Egyptians were pursuing their former captives, the Hebrews, they gave little thought to the power of God to deliver His children. Therefore, they approached the Red Sea with a feeling of certainty that they would soon recapture their former slaves. God had different plans for His people, however. He told Moses to stretch his hand out over the sea so that a pathway of safe escape could be made for the Israelites. In this way, the followers of Moses made their way into the Promised Land, while the Egyptians drowned in the sea.

Filled with thanksgiving for God's mighty deliverance, Moses sang his prayer, "The Lord is my strength and my song; he has become my salvation. He is my God, and I will praise him, my father's God, and I will exalt him. The Lord is a warrior; the Lord is his name....Your right hand, O Lord, was majestic in power. Your right hand, O Lord, shattered the enemy. In the greatness of your majesty you threw down those who opposed you. You unleashed your burning anger; it consumed them like stubble....Who among the gods is like you, O Lord...? Who is like you — majestic in holiness, awesome in glory, working wonders?...The Lord will reign for ever and ever" (Exod. 15:2-18, NIV).

Moses literally sang this prayer of thanksgiving and praise. It was a time of worship for all the people. The children of Israel joined their leader in his song. Shortly afterward, Miriam, the prophetess, a sister of Aaron, began to lead the women in grateful dancing before the Lord. It was such a happy time. God had heard the cries of His people. As promised, He saw to it that they were delivered from their cruel oppressors. It was an appropriate occasion for rejoicing and worship.

Moses expressed profound adoration for the Lord in this prayer. He reflected on God's majesty, glory, holiness, and miracle-working power. He thanked God for His faithfulness, His goodness, His love. Prevailing prayers are prayers of thanksgiving, worship, and praise — joyful times when we recall all that God has done for us. The Psalmist echoes this theme: "Know that the Lord, He is God; It is He who has made us, and not we ourselves; We are His people, and the sheep of His pasture. Enter into His gates with thanksgiving, And into His courts with praise. Be thankful unto Him, and bless His name. For the Lord is good; His mercy is everlasting; And His truth endures to all generations" (Ps. 100:3-5, NKJV).

Solomon's Prayer for Wisdom

So many things stem from wisdom. Perhaps more than any other godly attribute, wisdom is needed in our daily lives. As God imparts wisdom to His servants, in response to their prayers, insights, discernment, truth, and victory are actualized in our lives. James wrote, "If any of you lacks wisdom, let him ask of God, who gives to all liberally and without reproach, and it will be given to him. But let him ask in faith, with no doubting, for he who doubts is like a wave of the sea driven and tossed by the wind. For let not that man suppose that he will receive anything from the Lord; he is a double-minded man, unstable in all his ways" (James 1:5-7, NKJV).

Solomon asked God for wisdom, and he became the wisest man on earth. The Book of Proverbs declares: "Happy is the man who finds wisdom, And the man who gains understanding; For her proceeds are better than the profits of silver, And her gain than fine gold. She is more precious than rubies, And all the things you may desire cannot compare with her. Length of days is in her right hand, In her left hand riches and honor. Her ways are ways of pleasantness, And all her paths are peace. She is a tree of life to those who take hold of her, And happy are all who retain her. The Lord by wisdom founded the earth; By understanding He established the heavens; By His knowledge the depths were broken up, And clouds drop down the dew" (Prov. 3:13-20, NKJV).

The blessings to be derived from the acquisition of wisdom are multitudinous. They include happiness, longevity, riches, honor, pleasantness, peace, life, etc. As a result of his prayer for wisdom, Solomon was able to enjoy these blessings and to lead countless others to them as well. The Lord appeared to Solomon in a dream and said, "Ask! What shall I give you?" (1 Kings 3:5, NKJV)

Solomon began his prayer by reflecting on the mercy God had extended to his father, David, then he thanked God for allowing him to become king after his father. He went on to say, "I know not how to go out or come in" (1 Kings 3:7). Realizing the importance of his royal position and responsibilities, Solomon prayed, "Therefore give to Your servant an understanding heart to judge Your people, that I may discern between good and evil. For who is able to judge this great people of Yours?" (1 Kings 3:9, NKJV).

Solomon's humble plea for wisdom and discernment greatly pleased the Lord who said, "Because you have asked this thing, and have not asked long life for yourself, nor have asked riches for yourself, nor have asked the life of your enemies, but have asked for yourself understanding to discern justice, behold, I have done according to your words; see, I have given you a wise and understanding heart, so that there has not been anyone like you before you, nor shall shall any like you arise after you.. And I have also given you what you have not asked: both riches and honor..." (1 Kings 3:11-13, NKJV).

Solomon prayed according to the will of God, and because of this, God moved quickly to grant his request — a request that was in full agreement with God's priorities and values. God always answers prayers that are congruent with His will; as a matter of fact, He delights in doing so.

The Book of Psalms

The Book of Psalms is a book of prayers. Most of these prayers are like songs, and many have been sung as aids to worship throughout the centuries. The Psalms include prayers of thanksgiving, intercession, adoration, praise, worship, and meditation. Often, the Psalmist (frequently David) prayed specifically for deliverance, guidance, forgiveness, protection, knowledge, wisdom, hope, God's constant love and care, and several other specific issues that affected his life. Most of the Psalms incorporate thanksgiving — an essential component of all effective prayer.

Because trust is the foundation block upon which our relationship with God is built, let us examine Psalm 62 — a prayer of trust — in which we discover many of the essential dynamics of the life of prevailing prayer. David begins, "Truly my soul silently waits for God; From Him comes my salvation" (Ps. 62:1, NKJV). David recognizes that God is his source for everything. He reflects on the fact that God is his Savior. This meditational style of prayer is most effective in that it helps us to see God in all of His majesty and glory, and this is the best possible way to begin our prayers. By meditating upon who God is as well as all that He has done for us, we are led into thanksgiving, praise, and worship in spirit and in truth. (See John 4:22-24.)

This moment of reflection and meditation at the outset of David's prayer of trust leads him to see God as his rock of security. "He only is my rock and my salvation; he is my defence; I shall not be greatly moved" (Ps. 62:2). Already, this man of prayer finds that his levels of trust in God are increasing. He goes on, "My soul, wait silently for God alone; For my expectation is from Him" (Ps. 62:5, NKJV). God is David's source — his only source. David refuses to be moved from the place of security, confidence, and trust he finds in God, because he knows, "In God is my salvation and my glory: the rock of my strength, and my refuge, is in God" (Ps. 62:7).

The process of praying brings the very answers David needs directly to his heart. This is a wonderful miracle of prayer. Notice how he turns his prayer into a marvelous proclamation of complete and unswerving trust in God: "Trust in Him at all times, you people; Pour out your heart before Him; God is a refuge for us" (Ps. 62:8, NKJV). Through prayer, David is no longer concerned about his own needs. He has received his answer — God is "the rock of my strength, and my refuge" (Ps. 62:7). Sometimes that is enough for us to know. It is knowledge that is derived through prayer and meditation upon the Word of God. Through prayer, David is able to take charge of his soul. In fact, he commands his soul, "My soul, wait silently for God alone; For my expectation is from Him" (Ps. 62:5, NKJV). Prayer gave David the strength to get control of his emotions. Now he was ready to minister to others in the same truth and trust he had received through prayer.

He told the people to trust in God, not in oppression. He further encouraged them not to set their hearts upon riches — but to trust solely in God. His conclusion to Psalm 62 is a stirring tribute to the mercy and power of God — two qualities David was reassured of through prayer: "Power belongs to God. Also to You, O Lord, belongs mercy; For You render to each one according to his work" (Ps. 62:11-12, NKJV).

David had clearly set his heart to wait upon God. This is a major theme in the Book of Psalms, and it speaks of patience, trust, confidence, and hope. The avenue to these blessings, as David knew so well, was prayer.

Jonah's Prayer for Deliverance

Though most of us will probably not find ourselves in the same circumstances as Jonah (in the belly of a whale!), all of us have experienced the dilemmas associated with self-defeating behaviors such as avoiding God's will, trying to do our own thing instead of the right thing, and failing to fulfill our responsibilities. At such times, like Jonah, we've probably ended up in various degrees of difficulty. Such situations call for a prayerful response as we see exemplified in the story of Jonah.

"From inside the fish Jonah prayed to the Lord his God. He said: 'In my distress I called to the Lord, and he answered me. From the depths of the grave I called for help, and you listened to my cry. You hurled me into the deep, into the very heart of the seas, and the currents swirled about me; all your waves and breakers swept over me....the deep surrounded me; seaweed was wrapped around my head. To the roots of the mountains I sank down; the earth beneath barred me in forever. But you brought my life up from the pit, O Lord my God. When my life was ebbing away, I remembered you, Lord, and my prayer rose to you, to your holy temple" (Jon. 2:1-7, NIV).

Jonah began his prayer by reviewing the circumstances in which he found himself. He acknowledged his personal responsibility in all that had transpired: "They that observe lying vanities forsake their own mercy" (Jon. 2:8). Personal confession such as this is absolutely essential to all effective prayer. Jonah knew the truth that God had revealed to David, "If I regard iniquity in my heart, the Lord will not hear me" (Ps. 66:18).

Jonah repented of his sins of omission and commission, and then his prayer turned from one of supplication to one of thanksgiving. He was forgiven! "But I, with a song of thanksgiving, will sacrifice to you. What I have vowed I will make good. Salvation comes from the Lord" (Jon. 2:9, NIV). God heard his prayer, and He was pleased. The divine answer followed: "And the Lord commanded the fish, and it vomited out Jonah onto dry land" (Jon. 2:10, NIV).

The keys to getting his prayer of deliverance answered were trust, confession, thanksgiving, and repentance. Jonah prayed, God heard, and a wonderful miracle took place. Even while he was in the belly of the fish, Jonah was able to thank God for His blessings in his life. Soon after his deliverance, Jonah heard God's voice a second time, and the will of the Lord for his life was revealed unto him: "Go to the great city of Nineveh and proclaim to it the message I give you" (Jon. 3:2, NIV). Jonah didn't question God this time; he purposed in his heart to follow wherever He led.

The Church's Prayer in the Face of Threats

When the Church of Jesus Christ was young, martyrdom, persecution, imprisonment, and other tribulations were to be expected just as they are in many parts of the world today. Many felt threatened by the believers, and they reacted with growing animosity. The priests, Pharisees, and Sadducees were among the company of persecutors.

Peter and John, however, were bold proclaimers of the Gospel of Jesus Christ. They preached, "Nor is there salvation in any other, for there is no other name under heaven given among men by which we must be saved" (Acts 4:12, NKJV). The Jewish leaders conferred among themselves, and "they took knowledge of them, that they had been with Jesus" (Acts 4:13). Though they were impressed with the zeal and boldness of these disciples, the leaders did not know what to do about them. They wondered, "What shall we do to these men?" (Acts 4:16).

After their conference, the leaders determined to threaten Peter and John, and all the Christians, by forbidding them to teach and preach in the name of Jesus. Their threat was implied, not direct, but it was clear that the non-Christian religious leaders had severe punishment on their minds. Their greatest concern was with regard to how the general populace would react to the punishment. The people had seen miracles accomplished through the power of Jesus' name, and many glorified God for what they had seen. Therefore, the leaders simply threatened them.

The Church responded appropriately — through prayer. They united in and through prayer: "Lord, You are God, who made heaven and earth and the sea, and all that is in them, who by the mouth of Your servant David have said: 'Why did the nations rage, And the people plot vain things?'... Now, Lord, look on their threats, and grant to Your servants that with all boldness they may speak Your word, by stretching out Your hand to heal, and that signs and wonders may be done through the name of Your holy Servant Jesus" (Acts 4:24-25, 29, NKJV). The believers did not pray that they would be able to escape the persecution; instead, the focus of their prayers was that God would enable them to minister more powerfully! Their prayer was not selfish; it was Christ-centered, and it reflected the love of Jesus for people everywhere.

The miraculous results of their prayer changed the Church and the world for all time. Notice what happened: "And when they had prayed, the place where they were

assembled together was shaken; and they were all filled
with the Holy Spirit, and they spoke the word of God with
boldness. Now the multitude of those who believed were
of one heart and of one soul; neither did anyone say that
any of the things he possessed was his own, but they had
all things in common. And with great power the apostles
gave witness to the resurrection of the Lord Jesus. And
great grace was upon them all. Nor was there anyone
among them who lacked; for all who were possessors of
lands or houses sold them, and brought the proceeds of the
things that were sold, and laid them at the apostles' feet;
and they distributed to each as anyone had need" (Acts
4:31-35, NKJV).

Believing prayer, according to the Word of God,
resulted in the infilling of the Holy Spirit, unity among the
believers, boldness to speak the Word of God, spiritual
power, great grace, and the supply of every need. It has the
same results and blessings today!

Paul's Prayer of Thanksgiving

The Apostle Paul most often prayed intercessory
prayers for his fellow-believers. He prayed for the Roman
believers, for Israel, for the Corinthians, for Timothy, and
for Philemon. He prayed for the members of each of the
churches he established on his missionary journeys. Paul
was a true prayer warrior, and we can learn much from his
life of prayer.

When he wrote his letter to the Ephesian Christians,
Paul included a prayer of thanksgiving that is memorable
in so many important respects. He told them that he never

ceased making mention of them in his intercessions. He assured them he was thankful for them, and he shared the contents of those prayers with them: "I keep asking that the God of our Lord Jesus Christ, the glorious Father, may give you the Spirit of wisdom and revelation, so that you may know him better. I pray also that the eyes of your heart may be enlightened in order that you may know the hope to which he has called you, the riches of his glorious inheritance in the saints, and his incomparably great power for us who believe. That power is like the working of his mighty strength, which he exerted in Christ when he raised him from the dead and seated him at his right hand in the heavenly realms, far above all rule and authority, power, and dominion, and every title that can be given, not only in this present age, but also in the one to come. And God placed all things under his feet and appointed him to be head over everything for the church, which is his body, the fullness of him who fills everything in every way" (Eph. 1:17-23, NIV).

Paul was thankful for his fellow-believers. He wanted them to experience all God had in store for them — the spirit of wisdom and revelation, the knowledge of God, enlightened understanding, the hope of God's calling, the riches of the glory of God's inheritance, the greatness of His power, etc. In short, Paul wanted the Ephesians to know the fullness of God. This was his prayer for them because he loved them.

Later (in Ephesians 3), the Great Apostle prayed that they would know the love of Christ, and he concluded the chapter with this benediction: "Now to him who is able to do immeasurably more than all we ask or imagine, according to his power that is at work within us, to him be glory

in the church and in Christ Jesus throughout all generations, for ever and ever! Amen" (Eph. 3:20-21, NIV).

Paul was a prayer warrior. We can learn much from
his style of praying. His prayers were deeply spiritual and
they stemmed from his intimate relationship with God. In
fact, his prayers reveal the spiritual closeness he had with
his heavenly Father. The entire book of Ephesians can be
paraphrased as a personalized prayer for every believer to
pray for himself and others. The words are powerful faith-
building truths that form a strong framework for personal
prayer.

In your daily quiet time, take a chapter of Ephesians
and restyle it as a personal prayer. God always responds to
His Word because His Word contains His will. This
process fortifies the believer with the truth of the Bible,
enabling the believer to focus on God's promises instead of
the problems of life. Imagine the exciting dimensions of a
prayer that is formed by these words of Paul (from
Ephesians 2): "Heavenly Father, I was once dead in my
trespasses and sins, but you have extended your grace to
me, and you have quickened me and set me free! I used to
walk according to the course of this world, according to the
prince of the power of the air, the spirit that now works in
the children of disobedience. I used to walk with them as
well, according to the lusts of my flesh and fulfilling the
desires of my flesh and the desires of my mind. By nature,
Father, I was a child of wrath, even as other people are
today. But you, Lord, the One who is so rich in mercy,
loved me with your great love, and you saved me even
when I was dead in my sins. You extended your grace to
me, and now you have raised me up and have enabled me
to sit in heavenly places with Christ Jesus, my Lord. I

know your purpose for my life is to show the exceeding riches of your grace...."

The preceding prayer was paraphrased from the first seven verses of Ephesians 2. Truly, the same approach of praying the Scriptures may be applied to the entire book of Ephesians with wonderful results. This dynamic method of prayer is the basis of the topical prayers of this book. We pray that this style of praying personal prayers based on the Word of God will revolutionize your praying and your life so that Paul's prayer for the Ephesians will be your portion as well. Our prayer for you is:

We pray that God, out of His glorious riches, will strengthen you with power through His Spirit in your inner being so that Christ may dwell in your heart by faith. And we pray that you, being rooted and established in love, may have power, together with all the saints, to grasp how wide and long and high and deep is the love of Christ, and to know this love that surpasses knowledge — that you may be filled to the measure of all the fullness of God. (Eph. 3:16-19, authors' paraphrase)

Reflections on Prayer

As for me, I will call upon God; and the Lord shall save me. Evening, and morning, and at noon, will I pray, and cry aloud: and he shall hear my voice. (Ps. 55:16-17)

Reuben Archer Torrey

"We need to pray...because of what prayer accomplishes....Prayer promotes our spiritual growth....Prayer also brings power into our work....Prayer avails for the conversion of others....Prayer brings blessings to the Church....It was so in the days of Knox. It was so in the days of Edwards and Brainerd. It was so in the days of Finney. It was so in the days of the great revival of 1857 in this country and of 1859 in Ireland. And, it will be so again in your day and mine!" (From *How to Pray* by R.A. Torrey).

Watch therefore, and pray always that you may be counted worthy to escape all these things that will come to pass, and to stand before the Son of Man. (Luke 21:36, NKJV)

"Prayers are hindered by unbelief. God demands that we believe His Word absolutely. To question it is to make Him a liar. Many of us do that when we plead His promises.

Is it any wonder that our prayers are not answered? How many prayers are hindered by our wretched unbelief! We go to God and ask Him for something that is positively promised in His Word, and then we only half expect to get it. 'Let not that man think that he shall receive any thing of the Lord.'" (From *How to Pray* by R.A. Torrey).

> *If any of you lacks wisdom, let him ask of God, who gives to all liberally and without reproach, and it will be given to him. But let him ask in faith, with no doubting, for he who doubts is like a wave of the sea driven and tossed by the wind. For let not that man suppose that he will receive anything from the Lord; he is a double-minded man, unstable in all his ways. (James 1:5-8, NKJV)*

"There is mighty power in prayer. It has much to do with our obtaining fullness of power in Christian life and service. Whoever will not take time for prayer may as well give up all hope of obtaining the fullness of power God has for him" (From *How to Obtain Fullness of Power* by R.A. Torrey).

> *But those who wait on the Lord Shall renew their strength; They shall mount up with wings like eagles; They shall run and not be weary, They shall walk and not faint. (Isa. 40:31, NKJV)*

Edward McKendree Bounds

"Prayer is absolutely dependent upon faith. Virtually, it has no existence apart from it, and accomplishes nothing unless it be its inseparable companion. Faith makes prayer effectual, and in a certain important sense, must precede it" (From *The Necessity of Prayer* by E.M. Bounds).

> *For assuredly, I say to you, whosoever says to this mountain, 'Be removed, and be cast into the sea,' and does not doubt in his heart, but believes that those things he says will be done, he will have whatever he says.*
>
> *(Mark 11:23, NKJV)*

"The requisites of true prayer are the requisites of scriptural, vital, personal religion. They are the requisites of real religious service in this life. Primary among these requisites is that in serving, we serve. So in praying, we must pray. Truth and heart reality, these are the core, the substance, the sum, the heart of prayer. There are no possibilities in prayer without we really pray in all simplicity, reality and trueness" (From *Prayer and Praying Men* by E.M. Bounds).

> *Then you shall call, and the Lord will answer; You shall cry, and He will say, 'Here I am.'...The Lord will guide you continually, And satisfy your soul in drought, And strengthen your bones; You shall be like a watered garden, And like a spring of water, whose waters do not fail. (Isa. 58:9, 11, NKJV)*

Jonathan Edwards

"When a boy, I used to pray five times a day in secret, and to spend much time in religious conversation with other boys. I used to meet with them to pray together. So it is God's will through His wonderful grace, that the prayers of His saints should be one great and principal means of carrying on the designs of Christ's kingdom in the world" (From *The Diary of Jonathan Edwards*).

> *If you ask anything in My name, I will do it. (John 14:14, NKJV)*

"Resolved to exercise myself in this all my life long, with the greatest openness to declare my ways to God, and to lay my soul open to God — all my sins, temptations, difficulties, sorrows, fears, hopes, desires, and everything and every circumstance" (From *The Diary of Jonathan Edwards*).

> *Now to Him who is able to do exceedingly abundantly above all that we ask or think, according to the power that works in us. (Eph. 3:20, NKJV)*

Andrew Murray

"A life abiding in Christ and filled with the Spirit, a life entirely given up as a branch for the work of the vine, has the power to claim these promises, and to pray the effectual prayer that avails much. Lord, teach us to pray" (From *The Ministry of Intercession* by Andrew Murray).

> *If you abide in Me, and My words abide in you, you will ask what you desire, and it shall be done for you. (John 15:7, NKJV)*

"Do you not see how all depends on God and prayer? As long as He lives, loves, hears, and works, as long as there are souls with hearts closed to the Word, as long as there is work to be done in carrying the Word — pray without ceasing. Continue steadfastly in prayer, watching therein with thanksgiving. These are words for every Christian" (From *The Ministry of Intercession* by Andrew Murray).

> *God be merciful unto us, and bless us; and cause his face to shine upon us. (Ps. 67:1)*

"Little of the Word with little prayer is death to the spiritual life. Much of the Word with little prayer gives a sickly life. Much prayer with little of the Word gives more life, but without steadfastness. A full measure of the Word and prayer each day gives a healthy and powerful life" (From *The Prayer Life* by Andrew Murray).

> *But we will give ourselves continually to prayer. (Acts 6:4)*

"Our life has a great influence on our prayer, just as in the same way our prayer influences our life. The entire life of man is a continuous prayer, to nature or to the world, to provide for his wants and make him happy. This natural prayer and desire of the heart can be so strong in a man who also prays to God that the words of prayer which his mouth utters cannot be heard. At times God cannot hear the prayer of your lips because the desires of your heart after the world cry out to Him much more strongly and loudly" (From *The Prayer Life* by Andrew Murray).

> *You ask, and you do not receive, because you ask amiss, that you may spend it on your pleasures. (James 4:3, NKJV)*

"God lives and listens to every petition with His whole heart. Each time we pray, the whole infinite God is there to hear. He asks that in each prayer the whole man be there, too. He asks that we cry with our whole heart. Christ gave himself to God for men. And so, He takes up every need into His intercession. If once we seek God with our whole heart, the whole heart will be in every prayer with which we come to God. Pray with your whole heart" (From *The Ministry of Intercession* by Andrew Murray).

> *Continue in prayer, and watch in the same with thanksgiving. (Col. 4:2)*

"Prayer is not monologue, but dialogue; God's voice in response to mine is its most essential part. Listening to God's voice is the secret of the assurance that He will listen to mine" (Andrew Murray).

> *Blessed be the Lord, Because He has heard the voice of my supplications! (Ps. 28:6, NKJV)*

"Beware in your prayer, above everything, of limiting God, not only by unbelief, but by fancying that you know what He can do" (Andrew Murray).

> *But know that the Lord has set apart for Himself him who is godly; The Lord will hear when I call to Him. (Ps. 4:3, NKJV)*

"Get linked to God. Adore and trust Him as the omnipotent One, not only for your own life, but for all the souls that are entrusted to you. Never pray without adoring His omnipotence, saying, 'Mighty God, I claim your almightiness.' And the answer to the prayer will come. Like Abraham you will become strong in faith, giving glory to

God, because you account Him who has promised able to perform" (From *Absolute Surrender* by Andrew Murray).

And he said, The things which are impossible with men are possible with God. (Luke 18:27)

Lady Maxwell of Edinburgh

"Of late I feel painfully convinced that I do not pray enough. Lord, give me the spirit of prayer and supplication. Oh, what a cause of thankfulness is it that we have a gracious God to whom to go on all occasions! Use and enjoy this privilege and you can never be miserable. Who gives thanks for this royal privilege? It puts God in everything, His wisdom, power, control and safety. Oh, what an unspeakable privilege is prayer! Let us give thanks for it. I do not prove all the power of prayer that I wish" (From *The Diary of Lady Maxwell*).

And there is no one who calls on Your name, Who stirs himself up to take hold of You. (Isa. 64:7, NKJV)

William Law

"When you begin your petitions use such various expressions of the attributes of God as may make you most sensible of the greatness and power of the divine nature" (From *Devout Life* by William Law).

Call to Me, and I will answer you, and show you great and mighty things, which you do not know. (Jer. 33:3, NKJV)

Samuel Chadwick

"Go back! back to that upper room; back to your knees; back to searching of heart and habit, thought and life; back to pleading, praying, waiting, till the Spirit of the Lord floods the soul with light, and you are endued with power from on high. Then go forth in the power of Pentecost, and the Christ-life shall be lived, and the works of Christ shall be done. You shall open blind eyes, cleanse foul hearts, break men's fetters, and save men's souls. In the power of the indwelling Spirit, miracles become the commonplace of daily living" (Source unknown).

> *Draw nigh to God, and he will draw nigh to you. (James 4:8)*

Dwight L. Moody

"Faith is taking God at His Word. Those who want some sign are always getting into trouble. We want to come to this: God says it — let us believe it" (From *The Way to God* by D. L. Moody).

> *So then faith comes by hearing, and hearing by the word of God. (Rom. 10:17, NKJV)*

"Thank God, we can come under His banner today if we want to. His banner of love is over us....Let the love of God be shed abroad in your heart by the Holy Spirit today. It will drive away darkness and gloom. It will drive away sin, and peace and joy will be yours" (From *The Way to God* by D.L. Moody).

*He brought me to the banqueting house, and his
banner over me was love. (Song of Sol. 2:4)*

"Spread out your petition before God, and then say,
'Thy will, not mine, be done.' The sweetest lesson I have
learned in God's school is to let the Lord choose for me"
(From the writings of Dwight L. Moody).

*I will call upon the Lord, who is worthy to
be praised; So shall I be saved from my enemies.
(2 Sam. 22:4, NKJV)*

Martin Luther

"To pray well is the better half of study" (From the
writings of Martin Luther).

*He who calls you is faithful, who also will
do it. (1 Thess. 5:24, NKJV)*

"Prayer is a strong wall and fortress of the church; it
is a goodly Christian weapon" (From the writings of
Martin Luther).

Pray without ceasing. (1 Thess. 5:17)

Brother Lawrence

"We ought to act with God in the greatest simplicity,
speaking to Him frankly and plainly, and imploring His
assistance in our affairs, just as they happen" (From *The
Practice of the Presence of God* by Brother Lawrence).

> *Let us therefore come boldly unto the throne of grace, that we may obtain mercy, and find grace to help in time of need. (Heb. 4:16)*

Phillips Brooks

"O, do not pray for easy lives. Pray to be stronger men. Do not pray for tasks equal to you powers. Pray for powers equal to your tasks" (From *Going Up to Jerusalem* by Phillips Brooks).

> *For all the promises of God in Him are Yes, and in Him Amen, to the glory of God through us. (2 Cor. 1:20, NKJV)*

John Bunyan

"He who runs from God in the morning will scarcely find Him the rest of the day" (From the writings of John Bunyan).

> *Submit yourselves therefore to God.*
> *(James 4:7)*

"Prayer is a sincere, sensible, affectionate pouring out of the soul to God, through Christ in the strength and assistance of the Spirit, for such things as God has promised" (From the writings of John Bunyan).

> *Is any thing too hard for the Lord?*
> *(Gen. 18:14)*

"When thou prayest, rather let thy heart be without words than thy words without heart" (From the writings of John Bunyan).

Your Father knows the things you have need of before you ask Him. (Matt. 6:8, NKJV)

Francois de Salignac de la Mothe Fenelon

"To pray...is to desire; but it is to desire what God would have us desire. He who desires not from the bottom of his heart, offers a deceitful prayer" (From *Advice Concerning Prayer* by Fenelon).

He hears the cry of the afflicted.
(Job 34:28, NKJV)

"He who prays without confidence cannot hope that his prayers will be granted" (From *Maximes: on Prayer* by Fenelon).

He does not forget the cry of the humble.
(Ps. 9:12, NKJV)

Soren Kierkegaard

"Prayer does not change God, but changes him who prays" (From the writings of Soren Kierkegaard).

They looked to Him and were radiant, And their faces were not ashamed. (Ps. 34:5, NKJV)

Charles Haddon Spurgeon

"Prayers are heard in heaven very much in proportion to our faith. Little faith will get very great mercies, but great faith still greater" (From *Gleanings Among the Sheaves: Believing Prayer* by Charles Haddon Spurgeon).

> *Trust in the Lord with all your heart.*
> *(Prov. 3:5, NKJV)*

"He [Jesus] is always to be found in the thickest part of the battle. When the wind blows cold He always takes the bleak side of the hill. The heaviest end of the cross lies ever on His shoulders. If He bids us carry a burden, He carries it also. If there is anything that is gracious, generous, kind, and tender, yea, lavish and superabundant in love, you always find it in Him. His service is life, peace, joy. Oh, that you would enter on it at once! God help you to enlist under the banner of Jesus Christ!" (From C.H. Spurgeon's last sermon in the Metropolitan Tabernacle pulpit).

> *For everyone who asks receives, and he who seeks finds. (Matt. 7:8, NKJV)*

Selected Quotations and Scriptures on Prayer

"The cultivation of the inner life requires withdrawal, solitude, quiet moments of being alone with God in prayer and communion" (Anonymous).

> *The Lord is near to all who call upon Him, To all who call upon Him in truth.*
> *(Ps. 145:18, NKJV)*

"Prayer does not consist in battering the walls of heaven for personal benefits or the success of our plans;

rather, it is the committing of ourselves for the carrying out of His purposes" (Anonymous).

> *Then you will call upon Me and go and pray to Me, and I will listen to you.*
>
> *(Jer. 29:12, NKJV)*

"Prayer is not to ask what we wish of God, but what He wishes of us" (Anonymous).

> *Be anxious for nothing, but in everything by prayer and supplication, with thanksgiving, let your requests be made known to God; and the peace of God, which surpasses all understanding, will guard your hearts and minds through Christ Jesus.*
>
> *(Phil. 4:6-7, NKJV)*

"The wings of prayer carry high and far" (Anonymous).

> *Verily, verily, I say unto you, whatsoever ye shall ask the Father in my name, he will give it you. (John 16:23).*

"In the morning, prayer is the key that opens to us the treasures of God's mercies and blessings; in the evening, it is the key that shuts us up under His protection and safeguard" (Anonymous).

> *Lord, teach us to pray. (Luke 11:1)*

"Prayer changes things; praise keeps what prayer has changed" (Anonymous).

I will therefore that men pray every where, lifting up holy hands, without wrath and doubting. (1 Tim. 2:8)

"Minutes spent with the Master in the morning may mean hours of blessing for the rest of the day" (Anonymous).

And whatever you ask in My name, that I will do, that the Father may be glorified in the Son. If you shall ask anything in My name, I will do it. (John 14:13-14, NKJV)

"Things begun in prayer usually end in power" (Anonymous).

For to be carnally minded is death; but to be spiritually minded is life and peace.
(Rom. 8:6)

More Keys to Answered Prayer

In our first book, *Prayers That Prevail — the Believer's Manual of Prayers*, we presented ten keys to answered prayer. That list was by no means exhaustive, so we have combed the Scriptures for ten additional keys that will help you to open the door to an increasingly adventurous life of prevailing prayer.

First, let's review the ten keys to answered prayer we discussed in our earlier volume. They are as follows:

> Key #1. *Praying According to the Will of God.* This is the foundation of all our prayer books. It is based upon the prayer promise found in 1 John 5:14-15: "Now this is the confidence that we have in Him, that if we ask anything according to His will, He hears us. And if we know that He hears us, whatever we ask, we know that we have the petitions that we have asked of Him" (NKJV).

> Key #2. *Praying in the Name of Jesus.* Jesus is the name that is above every name, and He promises, "If you ask

anything in My name, I will do it"
(John 14:14, NKJV).

Key #3. *Praying in Faith, Nothing Wavering.*
God rewards our faith. Jesus promises,
"Therefore I say to you, whatever things
you ask when you pray, believe that you
receive them, and you will have them"
(Mark 11:24, NKJV).

Key #4. *Persistence in Prayer.* It is the
"effectual, fervent prayer" of the righteous that avails much. (See James
5:16.) The Apostle Paul writes, "Pray
without ceasing" (1 Thess. 5:17).

Key #5. *Being Specific in Prayer.* Prayer
helps us to focus on the things that we
should be praying for, and Jesus
promises, "For assuredly, I say to you,
whoever says to this mountain, 'Be
removed and be cast into the sea,' and
does not doubt in his heart, but
believes that those things he says will
be done, he will have whatever he
says" (Mark 11:23, NKJV).

Key #6. *Praying in Humility.* Brokenness
before the Lord, and its resulting
humility, are true keys to answered
prayer: "The sacrifices of God are a
broken heart spirit, A broken and a
contrite heart — These, O God, You
will not despise" (Ps. 51:17, NKJV).

Key #7. *Praying in the Spirit.* The Holy Spirit is a Spirit of prayer. "Likewise the Spirit also helps in our weaknesses. For we do not know what we should pray for as we ought, but the Spirit Himself makes intercession for us with groanings which cannot be uttered" (Rom. 8:26, NKJV).

Key #8. *Waiting on God.* Patience is an integral component of prevailing prayer because God's timing is always perfect. "But let patience have its perfect work, that you may be perfect and complete, lacking nothing" (James 1:4, NKJV).

Key #9. *Thanksgiving and Praise.* These keys open the door to God's throne room where the true believer finds fullness of joy and pleasures forever. "Enter into his gates with thanksgiving, and into his courts with praise: be thankful unto him, and bless his name" (Ps. 100:4).

Key #10. *Abiding in Christ.* Abiding in Christ brings answers to our prayers, as our Lord Jesus pointed out: "If you abide in Me, and My words abide in you, you will ask what you desire, and it shall be done for you" (John 14:7, NKJV).

The above keys present practical precepts and principles to follow in building your prayer life. As you pray, keep the promises of God in your mind. This will renew your thought processes, revitalize your faith, and provide you with hope, spiritual vitality, and an expectant heart. Countless other blessings will result as well.

The Scriptures are replete with examples of the power of prayer. Each of the prophets and apostles admonishes us to pray regularly, with faith and confidence. Let's add the following keys to answered prayer to our key ring that is derived from their scriptural admonitions.

Key #11 — **ABSOLUTE SURRENDER**

Who is the Lord of your life? In the earthly realm, a lord is one who has absolute control over his domain. In fact, his servants are required to obey him and serve him with all they have and are. It is precisely the same in the spiritual realm. The Apostle Paul wrote, "You were bought at a price. Therefore honor God with your body" (1 Cor. 6:20, NIV). The price Paul refers to is the blood of Christ that was shed to redeem mankind.

This surrender of our lives to Christ is a prerequisite for power in prayer. Andrew Murray writes, "The condition for obtaining God's full blessing is *absolute surrender* to Him" (From *Absolute Surrender* by Andrew Murray). Surrendering our lives to God implies an absolute surrender to His will and a firm belief that He always knows what is best for us.

Jesus modeled this attitude for all of us when He prayed so fervently in the Garden of Gethsemane: "Father, if you are willing, take this cup from me; yet not my will, but yours, be done" (Luke 22:42, NIV).

Likewise, Job surrendered his life and everything he owned to God. He proclaimed, "Though he slay me, yet will I trust in him" (Job 13:15). Job believed in the power of prayer, and he prevailed in prayer. After surrendering everything to his Lord — including his life itself — he developed an intimate relationship with God through prayer. Job became an intercessor who learned how to count his blessings instead of his losses, and God richly rewarded him: "And the Lord turned the captivity of Job, when *he prayed for his friends*: also the Lord gave Job twice as much as he had before" (Job 42:10, italics ours).

God expects your surrender. He will help you to take the leap of faith that such a surrender requires. He will accept your surrendered heart as His prize possession. He will enable you to maintain your absolute surrender to Him, and He will bless you with answers to your prayers!

Key #12 — **REPENTANCE**

Repentance involves a commitment to turn away from sin and selfishness, to walk in complete obedience to Christ, and to yield our lives to His Lordship. Though sorrow and grief over our sins often accompany true repentance, it is our spiritual resolve rather than our emotional response that truly counts. Fortitude results from such a resolve to do God's will.

An individual who is fully repentant has given up all rights to his or her life, choosing to put God first in all things. Jesus said, "But seek first the kingdom of God and His righteousness, and all these things shall be added to you" (Matt. 6:33, NKJV). This powerful prayer promise is placed in the context of the disciples who were worrying whether their needs would be met. Jesus assured them, "Your heavenly Father knoweth that ye have need of all these things" (Matt. 6:32).

They were trying to figure things out by leaning on their own understanding, and Jesus rebuked them for their lack of faith. In effect, He called them to repentance from their worldliness and selfishness, and to turn to their heavenly Father who "sees in secret" and "will reward you openly" (Matt. 6:18, NKJV).

In order to prevail in prayer, therefore, we need to take these words of Jesus to heart by repenting of materialism and the tendency to look at things as the world views them. The author of the Book of Proverbs shows us how this can be accomplished: "Trust in the Lord with all thine heart; and lean not unto thine own understanding. In all thy ways acknowledge him, and he shall direct your paths" (Prov. 3:5-6).

Key #13 — **TRUSTING IN THE LORD**

Any true relationship, if it is to be effective, requires that the element of trust be incorporated into all its dynamics. Without trust there can be no commitment, another essential ingredient in every working relationship. God has given us hundreds of personal promises in His Word. To have a prevailing prayer life, we must trust God implicitly to fulfill His Word in our lives. As we learn to focus on His promises trustfully we begin to see Him move in response to our faith in His Word and His trustworthiness.

D.L. Moody wrote, "Just take God at His Word and trust His Son this very day, this very hour, this very moment....To believe on the Lord Jesus Christ is simply to take Him at His Word" (From *The Way to God* by D.L. Moody). Trusting in the Lord is taking Him at His Word. The prayers contained within this book are designed to help you to do exactly that by praying the Scriptures, thereby focusing on the promises of God as you pray.

> *"Oh, taste and see that the Lord is good; Blessed is the man who trusts in him!" (Ps. 34:8, NKJV).*

Key #14 — **A FORGIVING HEART**

Jesus said, "Therefore, if you are offering your gift at the altar and there remember that your brother has something against you, leave your gift there in front of the altar. First go and be reconciled to your brother; then come and offer your gift" (Matt. 5:23-24, NIV).

Christianity is best defined in terms of relationships — loving God with all our hearts and loving our neighbors as ourselves. Unforgiveness in any of these vital relationships blocks our access to God who commands us to "be ye kind and compassionate to one another, forgiving each other, just as in Christ God forgave you" (Eph. 4:32, NIV).

The model prayer of Jesus — the Lord's Prayer — reveals what the attitudes of our hearts should be: "And forgive us our debts, as we forgive our debtors" (Matt. 6:12). When we utter these words, it is advisable for us to remember the clear meaning of what we are praying. Do we really want God to forgive us in the same way we forgive others? If we do, it is imperative for us to be sure that we have forgiven all those who have wronged us. When we fail to do this, we open the door to bitterness and resentment — twin attitudes that lead to prayerlessness and powerlessness in prayer.

Jesus spells it out in vivid terms: "For if you forgive men when they sin against you, your heavenly Father will also forgive you. But if you do not forgive men their sins, your Father will not forgive your sins" (Matt. 6:14-15, NIV).

Key #15 — A FORGIVEN HEART

The Psalmist wrote, "If I regard iniquity in my heart, the Lord will not hear me" (Ps. 66:18). In the same way that a lack of forgiveness toward others hinders our prayer life, unconfessed sin in our lives prevents the Lord from hearing our prayers.

God had provided the remedy for all sin through His Son, the Lord Jesus Christ. The blood that Jesus shed on Calvary's cross cleanses us from all sin, and it enables us to have direct access to our Father in heaven. "If we confess our sins, he is faithful and just to forgive us our sins, and to cleanse us from all unrighteousness" (1 John 1:9).

R.A. Torrey wrote, "Sin hinders prayer. Perhaps a man prays and prays and receives no answer to his prayer....Anyone who finds his prayers unanswered should not think that what he asks of God is not according to His will. Instead, he should go alone to God with the Psalmist's prayer, 'Search me, O God, and know my heart: try me, and know my thoughts: and see if there be any wicked way in me' (Ps. 139:23-24)" (From *How to Pray* by R.A. Torrey).

You will know when your heart is not right with God. His Spirit will convict you of the areas you need to change, and those changes will be initiated by your personal confession. Hear the words of the prophet Isaiah: "Behold, the Lord's hand is not shortened, that it cannot save; neither his ear heavy, that it cannot hear: But your iniquities have separated between you and your God, and your sins have hid his face from you, that he will not hear" (Isa. 59:1-2).

God delights in forgiving His children when they come to Him in openness and confession. He always hears the prayers that flow from a believer's forgiven heart. Such prayers become true *Prayers That Prevail.*

Key #16 — **AGREEMENT**

We have already pointed out how agreement with God and His Word is the foundation on which an effectual prayer life is constructed. We must be certain that our prayers are in alignment with the will of God as it is revealed in the holy Scriptures. By praying the Scriptures and focusing on their promises, we can be certain that we are praying according to the will of God. (See 1 John 5:14-15.)

Another key to prevailing prayer involves agreement with our fellow-believers as well. Jesus said, "If two of you agree on earth concerning anything that they ask, it will be done for them by my Father in heaven. For where two or three are gathered together in My name, I am there in the midst of them" (Matt. 18:19-20, NKJV).

The power of agreement in prayer must not be minimized. Rhoda and her friends in the Book of Acts saw this truth revealed in a genuinely miraculous way: "Peter was therefore kept in prison, but *constant prayer was offered to God for him by the church*....And as Peter knocked at the door of the gate, a girl named Rhoda came to answer..." (Acts 12:5, 13, NKJV, italics ours). Their prayers had been answered by an angel who was sent by God to release Peter from prison. When the newly released prisoner arrived at the house of Mary, the mother of John, where the praying believers had gathered, there was total astonishment as the realization dawned upon them that their prayer of agreement had been answered!

The Apostle James confirms the power of the prayer of agreement: "Confess your trespasses to one another, and pray for one another, that you may be healed. The effective, fervent prayer of a righteous man avails much" (James 5:16, NKJV).

Let us be sure to agree with one another as we pray in agreement with God's Word and will. Such praying will always bring positive results!

Key #17 — **MEDITATING ON GOD'S WORD**

Like prayer, the Bible is a most practical tool and weapon in the hands of a believer. By meditating on the Word of God our faith is strengthened to enable us to appropriate God's promises for our life and the lives of others.

A godly person finds his or her delight "...in the law of the Lord, and on his law he meditates day and night. He is like a tree planted by the streams of water, which yields its fruit in season and whose leaf does not wither. Whatever he does prospers" (Ps. 1:2-3, NIV). Through meditation on the Scriptures a person learns to hide God's Word in his or her heart, and by doing so, the individual discovers answers for all of life's dilemmas.

Jesus promises, "If you abide in Me, *and My words abide in you*, you will ask what you desire, and it shall be done for you" (John 15:7, NKJV, italics ours). The words of the Lord find their abiding place in our hearts when we meditate upon them and apply them to our praying. This builds confidence in our hearts. It is as R.A. Torrey discloses, "Study the Word to find what God's will is as revealed there in the promises. Then, simply take these promises and claim them before God in prayer with the absolutely unwavering expectation that He will do what He has promised in His Word" (From *How to Pray* by R.A. Torrey).

As we learn to meditate upon the Word of God, all of our desires are transformed into realities. The Psalmist reveals how this happens in our lives: "Trust in the Lord and do good; dwell in the land and enjoy safe pasture. Delight yourself in the Lord and he will give you the desires of your heart. Commit your way to the Lord; trust in him and he will do this" (Ps. 37:3-5, NIV).

Key #18 — **GODLINESS**

As the will to become Christ-like grows strong in our hearts through prayer, studying His Word, Christian fellowship, and all other means of grace, we learn to see things from God's point of view and this changes everything in our lives. It transforms the way we pray, and it changes our values and priorities as well.

James writes, "Come near to God, and he will come near to you" (James 4:8, NIV). God draws us to himself so that we will become more like Him, sharing in His righteousness, holiness, and perfection. "We are His workmanship, created in Christ Jesus for good works, which God prepared beforehand that we should walk in them" (Eph. 2:10, NKJV). God is the Potter who is shaping our lives to conform to His will and image. (See Isa. 64:8 and Rom. 8:29.)

The closer we get to God, the more effective our praying will become. Paul wrote these words to young Timothy, "Godliness is profitable unto all things, having promise of the life that now is, and of that which is to come" (1 Tim. 4:8). As in all other things, godliness is profitable in our prayer lives. It is the source of both contentment and great gain, as Paul revealed to Timothy. A life of prayer leads to godliness, and godliness leads to power in prayer.

To be godly is to be like Christ who lived a life of prayer. When this goal becomes our greatest desire, we can expect answers to our prayers. "If our heart condemn us not, then we have confidence toward God. And whatsoever we ask, we receive of Him, because we obey His commandments, and do the things that are pleasing in His sight" (1 John 3:21).

Andrew Murray writes, "O my brethren! If you and I want to be like Jesus, we must especially contemplate Jesus praying alone in the wilderness. There is the secret of His wonderful life. What He did and spoke to man was first spoken and lived through the Father....Even though it might cost the sacrifice of night rest, of business, of fellowship with friends, the time must be found to be alone with the Father" (From *Like Christ* by Andrew Murray). In such sweet moments of communion we learn the secret of godliness that leads us to prevailing prayer.

Key #19 — **OBEDIENCE**

The Apostle John wrote these words, "And whatsoever we ask, we receive of him, because we keep his commandments, and do those things that are pleasing in his sight" (1 John 3:22). This verse helps us to see that many good things come to us when we give high priority to obeying God. We will receive answers to our prayers if we keep His commandments. Obedience is an important prerequisite to answered prayer.

There is a vast difference between knowing God's will and doing it. The Scriptures reveal His will to us, but we need to act upon His revealed will by applying His

Word to our lives and our praying. When we do this, we can be assured of the fact that God is listening and taking action in our behalf.

If we make it our heart-felt desire to please our Father in heaven, we can be sure that it will be His heart-felt desire to please us by answering our prayers. First, however, the gap between His ways and our ways, His thoughts and our thoughts, must be bridged by obedience to His will.

Key #20 — ACTIVE LISTENING

Prayer is a dialogue, not a monologue. Many prayers are like sermons, and some are like shopping lists. Others may be like gossip columns in a newspaper. Still others are eloquent speeches and discourses on the Scriptures. These approaches are not real prayers, however, for true prayer stems from an intimate relationship with the Father. He wants us to draw close to Him, and prayer is one of the avenues He has provided in order to make this possible.

God wants us to call out to Him, to even cry to Him if need be, but He also wants us to listen for His voice. Jesus said, "My sheep hear my voice, and I know them, and they follow me: And I give unto them eternal life; and they shall never perish" (John 10:27-28). If we call to God, we can be sure that He will answer us, but how will we know what the answer is unless we have disciplined ourselves through prayer and worship to know His voice?

By praying the Scriptures we are oftentimes praying the answers to our own prayers. God speaks to us through His Word and through the still, small voice of His Spirit.

Sometimes He speaks to us through circumstances as well. The important thing is to listen for His voice, and to follow up with a positive response to His will.

Isaiah, the prophet, shows what can happen in a believer's life when he or she prepares to hear the voice of God: "Your ears shall hear a word behind you, saying, 'This is the way, walk in it'" (Isa. 30:21, NKJV). Such words from God dispell all confusion, and they give us clear answers to our prayers. More importantly, the Word of God (the Bible) is always there to guide us into the Father's will.

Mary knew this key to answered prayer more fully than her sister, Martha, whom Jesus rebuked, "Martha, Martha, you are worried and troubled about many things. But one thing is needed, and Mary has chosen that good part, which will not be taken away from her" (Luke 10:41-42, NKJV).

What was "that good part"? It is worshiping at the Master's footstool where one learns to listen for the voice of God. He will speak to the hearts of those who love Him and want to learn to distinguish His voice from all others.

The faithful use of the twenty keys we've presented will result in an effective prayer life for every believer. They will open windows of insight and truth, and doors to heaven's treasure-house. In addition, they are keys to understanding God's Word and His will. Keep these important guidelines in mind as you use the topical prayers in this book as a framework for building your own life of scriptural prayer.

"Call to Me, and I will answer you, and show you great and mighty things, which you do not know" (Jer. 33:3, NKJV). God wants to answer your prayers, and He is ever "...able to do immeasurably more than all we ask or imagine, according to his power that is at work within us" (Eph. 3:20, NIV).

Our spiritual key ring now holds twenty keys that open our hearts to *Prayers That Prevail*:

1. Praying according to the will of God (His Word).
2. Praying in the name of Jesus.
3. Praying in faith, nothing wavering.
4. Persistence in prayer.
5. Being specific in prayer.
6. Praying in humility.
7. Praying in the Spirit.
8. Waiting on God.
9. Thanksgiving and Praise.
10. Abiding in Christ.
11. Absolute Surrender.
12. Repentance.
13. Trusting in the Lord.
14. A Forgiving Heart.
15. A Forgiven Heart.
16. Agreement.
17. Meditating on God's Word.
18. Godliness.
19. Obedience.
20. Active Listening.

These scriptural keys have been provided for our use so that we could enter the wonderful dimension of prevailing prayer. As you have probably noted, many of these principles are related to each other; however, each has its unique place in our prayer lives. Each one requires a committed response from us. God will guide you as you endeavor to put these keys to use in your prayer life, because His promise remains true: "Ask and it will be given to you; seek and you will find; knock and the door will be opened to you" (Matt. 7:7, NIV).

MORE PRAYERS THAT PREVAIL
(Topical Prayers From the Word of God)

Abundant Living

Key Thought: God wants to give you more than enough.

Key Scripture: *"I have come that they may have life, and that they may have it more abundantly" (John 10:10, NKJV).*

Prayer: Heavenly Father, thank you for the abundance you have provided for me in every area of my life. Truly, my cup overruns when I consider all that you have provided for me.[1] Thank you for supplying all my needs according to your riches in glory.[2] I believe the promises of your Word. All your promises are yes and amen.[3]

In my spirit, Lord, I hear the sound of the abundance of rain.[4] When I'm walking with you there always are showers of blessing in my life. Praise you, Father, for your goodness to me and for all the many blessings you've bestowed on me.

Give me meekness, Lord, so that I might follow in your steps and fulfill your promise that the meek will inherit the earth.[5] I believe your promise that I will be able to delight myself in the abundance of peace,[6] and in the abundance which flows from your hands.

Help me always to be aware of the fact that an individual's life does not consist of the abundance of things.[7] It will not profit me at all, Lord, if I gain the whole world and still lose my soul.[8] Teach me how to seek first your kingdom and your righteousness, for I know that by doing so I will find truly abundant living.[9]

I want to keep my focus clear at all times, Lord, so that I can see the relative values of spiritual and material things, realizing at all times that the things of the spirit are more precious than gold. I want to lay up treasures in heaven where moth and rust cannot corrupt and thieves cannot break in and steal.[10] By doing this, I know you will give me all that I need.

Thank you, Father, for the abundance of your grace.[11] I want to hold onto your abundance of joy at all times, Lord,[12] because I realize that your joy is my strength.[13]

Your grace, dear Father, is always sufficient for me.[14] Thank you for the power of prayer that builds my expectation and my hope and leads to the supply of your Spirit in my life.[15] According to my earnest expectation and my hope, I know that I will not be ashamed in anything.[16] For me, to live is Christ, and to die is gain.[17] Having godliness with contentment is great gain for me.[18] Thank you for all the blessings you have given to me in Christ Jesus.[19]

I praise you and glorify you for the abundant life you have imparted to me.[20]

References: *(1) Psalms 23:5; (2) Philippians 4:19; (3) 2 Corinthians 1:20; (4) 1 Kings 18:41; (5) Psalms 37:11; (6) Psalms 37:11; (7) Luke 12:15; (8) Luke 9:25; (9) Matthew 6:33; (10) Matthew 6:20; (11) Romans 5:17; (12) 2 Corinthians 8:2; (13) Nehemiah 8:10; (14) 2 Corinthians 12:9; (15) Philippians 1:19; (16) Philippians 1:20; (17) Philippians 1:21; (18) 1 Timothy 6:6; (19) Ephesians 1:3; (20) John 10:10.*

Achievement

Key Thought: There is no true achievement without the Lord.

Key Scripture: *"A good name is better than precious ointment"* *(Eccles. 7:1).*

Prayer: Dear Lord, help me to learn how to measure achievement in my life in the same way that you measure it. I want to do well,[1] to please you,[2] and to fully experience being accepted and received by you.[3] I want always to remember that unless you build the house, they who build it labor in vain.[4]

I delight to do your will, O God.[5] You have promised me that if I will delight myself in you, you will give me the desires of my heart.[6] Father, I want the desires of my heart to always be in line with yours at all times, for I know that desire accomplished is sweet to my soul and to you.[7] Through wisdom a house is built, and through understanding it is established.[8] Lord, I pray for your wisdom and understanding[9] so that I will be able to achieve your goals in my life.

There is nothing better than being able to rejoice in our own works, especially when those works have been guided and blessed by you.[10] As Jesus said, a person will be known by his fruits.[11] Lord, I want to be a fruitful

Christian. Continually fill me with your Spirit so that I will be able to bear the fruit of your Spirit in all the relationships and responsibilities of my life.[12] Help me to remember that true achievement is measured by the fruit of your Spirit: love, peace, joy, patience, meekness, gentleness, faithfulness, goodness, and self-control.[13] I want to bear such fruit in my life, Lord, and I know this will lead me to true achievement in every area of my life. Without Jesus, I can do nothing that really counts.[14] By abiding in Him, however, I will be able to bear much fruit in my life — the kind of fruit that lasts.[15] This is the kind of achievement I want, Father, and I know you want this for me as well.

When my journey is over, nothing would please me more than to hear you say, "Well done, good and faithful servant."[16] With Paul, I would like to be able to say, "I have fought a good fight, I have finished my course, I have kept the faith."[17] Father, you are the One who has built all things, and you continue to build your Kingdom on earth.[18] Help me to be your faithful co-laborer in all things.[19]

References: *(1) Genesis 4:7; (2) 1 Corinthians 7:32; (3) Romans 15:7; (4) Psalms 127:1; (5) Psalms 40:8; (6) Psalms 37:4; (7) Proverbs 13:19; (8) Proverbs 24:3; (9) James 1:5; (10) Ecclesiastes 3:24; (11) Matthew 7:20; (12) Ephesians 5:18; (13) Galatians 5:22-23; (14) John 15:5; (15) John 15:8; (16) Matthew 25:23; (17) 2 Timothy 4:7; (18) Hebrews 3:4; (19) Romans 8:17.*

Adjusting My Attitudes

Key Thought: The Beatitudes show us what our attitudes should be.

Key Scripture: *"Judge not, that you be not judged. For with what judgment you judge, you will be judged; and with the measure you use, it will be measured back to you. And why do you look at the speck in your brother's eye, but do not consider the plank in your own eye?" (Matt. 7:1-3, NKJV).*

Prayer: Heavenly Father, your Word renews my mind[1] and prayer changes the attitudes of my heart. I'm asking you to help me to adjust my attitudes in the following areas: _____

_____.

I want to get rid of all resentment and bitterness in my life, because I know a root of bitterness can spring up unexpectedly, thereby bringing defilement to many.[2]

Teach me your ways, Father, because I know your way is perfect. You are a mighty shield to all who trust in you.[3] Help me to trust you with all my heart instead of leaning upon my own understanding. In all my ways I will acknowledge you and I know you will direct my paths.[4]

I want my heart to be right before you at all times, Father.[5] Search my heart and thoughts, and point out anything in me that displeases you.[6] Cleanse me of all unrighteousness as I confess my wrong attitudes to you now.[7] I want to serve you in newness of spirit, not in the oldness of the letter.[8]   I want to be tender-hearted, learning to forgive as often as necessary those who wrong me.[9] Teach me how to bless those who curse me, to love my enemies, to do good to those who hate me, and to pray for those who despitefully use me and say all manner of evil against me.[10]

When I see someone overtaken in a fault, instead of judging or criticizing that person, I ask you to help me to restore him/her in the spirit of meekness, considering myself, lest I also be tempted.[11]   Thank you for pouring your love into my heart by your Holy Spirit[12] who enables me to reach out to others in love.

Father, I want my attitudes to be consistent with the fruit of the Spirit at all times. Help me to walk in the Spirit so that I will not fulfill the lusts of the flesh. Lead and strengthen me to walk in the fruit of love, joy, peace, patience, kindness, goodness, faithfulness, gentleness, and self-control. Father, I praise you for bringing forth this fruit in my life.[13]

References: *(1) Ephesians 4:23; (2) Hebrews 12:15; (3) Psalms 18:30; (4) Proverbs 3:5-6; (5) Acts 8:21; (6) Psalms 139:23; (7) 1 John 1:9; (8) Romans 7:6; (9) Ephesians 4:32; (10) Matthew 5:44; (11) Galatians 6:1; (12) Romans 5:5; (13) Galatians 5:16,22.*

Adonai
(The Lord Who Is Eternal)

Key Thought: "The created world is but a small parenthesis in eternity" (Sir Thomas Browne).

Key Scripture: *"The Lord shall reign for ever and ever"* *(Exod. 15:18).*

Prayer: Eternal Father, strong to save, I enter your presence with singing, and I go through your gates with thanksgiving.[1] I will serve you with gladness because I know that you are the Lord. You have created me and I am a sheep in your pasture. I bless your name, for you are good. Your mercy is everlasting and your truth endures to all generations.[2]

You are my God forever, and you will be my guide even unto death.[3] You will endure forever.[4] You are always the same, and your days will never end.[5] Your throne will remain from generation to generation,[6] and yours is the kingdom and the power and the glory forever.[7]

I thank you that I have the privilege of serving the God who is the eternal I AM,[8] the One who never changes.[9] I thank you for the security that comes from knowing that you are the same yesterday, today, and forever.[10] Every good and perfect gift comes from you, the Father of lights, with whom there is no variation or shadow of turning.[11] You, wonderful Lord, are the holy God of the universe; you always have been, you are now, and you always will be.[12] Praise your mighty name!

I call unto you with the certain knowledge that you will answer me.[13] You will be with me even unto the end of the age.[14] You will never leave me nor forsake me.[15] I do not present my supplications before you because of my righteousness, but I am able to do so because of your great mercies to me.[16] I thank you that you know what things I have need of even before I express them unto you.[17] I thank you that your eyes are always beholding me and your ears are open unto my prayers.[18]

I look forward to spending all eternity with you, Father. How I praise you for the gift of eternal life that I have obtained because your Son, my Lord and Savior, Jesus Christ, gave His life for me.[19] He gives me the victory.[20] Life with Him is both abundant and eternal.[21] Whosoever lives and believes in Him will never die.[22] Thank you, Lord, for loving me so much that you sent your Son to die for me.

References: *(1) Psalms 100:2,4; (2) Psalms 100:2-5; (3) Psalms 48:14; (4) Psalms 102:12; (5) Psalms 102:27; (6) Lamentations 5:19; (7) Matthew 6:13; (8) Exodus 3:14; (9) Malachi 3:6; (10) Hebrews 13:8; (11) James 1:17; (12) Revelation 4:8; (13) Psalms 34:17; (14) Matthew 28:20; (15) Hebrews 13:5; (16) Daniel 9:18; (17) Matthew 6:8; (18) 1 Peter 3:12; (19) Romans 6:23; (20) 1 Corinthians 15:57; (21) John 10:10; (22) John 11:26.*

Angelic Protection

Key Thought: Angels are watching over me.

Key Scripture: *"Be not forgetful to entertain strangers: for thereby some have entertained angels unawares" (Heb. 13:2).*

Prayer: Loving God, our heavenly Father, I thank you for angels, your messengers and our guardians.

Thank you for your promise that you give your angels charge over me, to keep me in all my ways, and that they lift me up in their hands to keep me from stumbling and falling.[1] In your heavenly realm there are thousands of chariots and tens of thousands of angels.[2] Thank you for the multitude of your heavenly host who excel in strength, who do your commandments, and who hearken to do your Word.[3] I praise you, Father, that the angel of the Lord encamps all around those who fear you, and delivers them.[4]

Lord, give your angels guardianship over my life so as to keep me in all your ways and deliver me from evil.[5] As your angels so faithfully ministered to the Lord Jesus, I pray that they will always be present to minister to my needs as well.[6] Thank you that your angels are ministering spirits who are sent forth by you to serve the heirs of salvation.[7] It gives me great comfort, Father, to realize that the angels who protect me are continually beholding your face in heaven,[8] and that innumerable company of angels is working in my behalf.[9]

Hasten the day, Lord, when Jesus shall send forth His angels to gather all things that offend out of His kingdom, including all those who work iniquity.[10] I look forward to the time when your angelic host will sever the wicked from among the just,[11] and the day the Son of Man comes in His glory, with all His holy angels.[12]

Thank you, Father, for giving Jesus a power that is far greater than the power of the angels, and thank you for giving Him a name that is more excellent than the name of angels.[13] I rejoice, and I praise you for His power, the power of His name, and the power of the angelic community of ministering spirits who worship you and serve your people.[14]

References: *(1) Psalms 91:11-12; (2) Psalms 68:17; (3) Psalms 103:20; (4) Psalms 34:7; (5) Psalms 91:11; (6) Matthew 4:11; (7) Hebrews 1:14; (8) Matthew 18:10; (9) Hebrews 12:22; (10) Matthew 13:41; (11) Matthew 13:49; (12) Matthew 25:31; (13) Hebrews 1:4; (14) Hebrews 1:7.*

Assurance of Salvation

Key Thought: Hallelujah! What a Savior!

Key Scripture: *"These things I have written to you who believe in the name of the Son of God, that you may know that you have eternal life, and that you may continue to believe in the name of the Son of God" (1 John 5:13, NKJV).*

Prayer: Father in heaven, thank you for sending your only begotten Son, Jesus Christ, to die for me so that by believing in Him I would be able to have assurance of the eternal life you provide to all those who love you.[1] Whosoever believes that Jesus is the Christ is born of you, Father.[2] Thank you for giving me the second birth so that I would never have to face the second death. Whosoever is born of you overcomes the world, and the victory that enables us to do so is the faith you impart to us.[3] I thank you for the certain knowledge that because I have been born again,[4] because I believe in your Son, that I shall truly overcome the world.[5]

I thank you for the love you have bestowed upon me, Father, that enables me to be called your child. I am thrilled to be your child, and I realize that it does not yet appear what I shall be, but I do know that, when Jesus comes again, I shall be like Him, and then I shall see Him as He is.[6] Praise your name, Father. I thank you that this hope within me purifies me.[7]

Help me to abide in Jesus, Father, because I know if I truly abide in Him, I will not sin.[8] I also know that if I will abide in Him, and let His words abide in me, I will be able to ask whatever I will, and it shall be done.[9] Whosoever is born of you, Father, does not commit sin.[10] Whosoever confesses that Jesus is the Son of God lives in you, and you live in him/her.[11]

Thank you for your gift of salvation, Father. I know it is not your will that any should perish, but that all should come to the knowledge of your salvation.[12] The wages of sin are death, but your free gift to all is eternal life.[13] Thank you for your rich grace that enables me to receive eternal life; it is your gift to me — not of works, lest I should boast.[14] Thank you for commending your love toward me in that while I was yet a sinner, Christ died for me.[15] I believe your Word. Because of this I confess with my mouth that Jesus Christ is my Lord and that you have raised Him from the dead; therefore, I know I am saved.[16] Thank you for so great a salvation, Lord.[17]

References: *(1) John 3:16; (2) 1 John 5:1; (3) 1 John 5:4; (4) 1 John 5:5; (5) 1 John 5:4; (6) 1 John 3:1-2; (7) 1 John 3:3; (8) 1 John 3:6; (9) John 15:7; (10) 1 John 3:9; (11) 1 John 4:15; (12) 2 Peter 3:9; (13) Romans 6:23; (14) Ephesians 2:8-9; (15) Romans 5:8; (16) Romans 10:9-10; (17) Hebrews 2:3.*

The Birth of a Baby

Key Thought: A baby is a bundle of divine potential.

Key Scripture: *"For this child I prayed, and the Lord has granted me my petition which I asked of Him. Therefore I also have lent him to the Lord; as long as he lives he shall be lent to the Lord" (1 Sam. 1:27-28, NKJV).*

Prayer: Heavenly Father, I come to you in celebration of the birth of_____.   Thank you for this child. Bless him/her, strengthen him/her, and guide him/her always.

It is wonderful to realize that children are an inheritance that we receive from you, and the fruit of the womb is a reward from you.[1] Thank you, Father, for children and for all the blessings they bring to us.

As arrows are in the hand of a mighty man, so are the children of one's youth. A parent who has a quiver full of children should be happy indeed.[2] May the parents of _____ recognize the wonderful blessing you have imparted unto them.

May this precious child be filled with wisdom, Lord, thereby making his/her father and mother glad.[3] Those who beget a wise child shall always have joy from him/her.[4] Teach _____ that true wisdom comes from honoring you.[5]

I pray that this child will receive Jesus Christ as his/her Lord and Savior at an early age,[6] and that he/she will always love you with all his/her heart, soul, mind, and strength and his/her neighbor as himself/herself.[7] I ask that he/she will have favor with God and mankind.[8]

I pray that he/she will be spiritually stalwart, mentally alert, and physically strong.[9] Give him/her a hunger for your Word, your righteousness, and your kingdom.[10] May he/she worship you in the beauty of holiness all the days of his/her life.[11]

Out of the mouths of babies you have perfected praise, Lord.[12] May this child love to praise you from an early age.

Prevent anyone from ever abusing this child. Keep him/her safe at all times. Let his/her guardian angel protect him/her, keeping watch over all his/her ways.[13]

Teach this child to love you, obey you, and to honor his/her parents throughout his/her life.[14] In so doing, Lord, I know it will be well with him/her and his/her days will be long upon the earth.[15]

References: *(1) Psalms 127:3; (2) Psalms 127:4-5; (3) Proverbs 15:20; (4) Proverbs 23:24; (5) Psalms 111:10; (6) John 1:12; (7) Mark 12:30-31; (8) Luke 2:52; (9) 2 Peter 1:3; (10) Matthew 6:33; (11) Psalms 29:2; (12) Matthew 21:16; (13) Psalms 34:7; (14) Ephesians 6:1; (15) Ephesians 6:2-3.*

The Blessings of God

Key Thought: The word "blessed" means happy and spiritually prosperous, experiencing God's favor.

Key Scripture: *"Behold, I set before you today a blessing and a curse: the blessing, if you obey the commandments of the Lord your God, which I command you today" (Deut. 11:26-27, NKJV).*

Prayer: Lord God, my loving heavenly Father, I come to you now with a heart filled with gratitude for all the blessings you have bestowed upon me. Thank you for blessing me and keeping me. Your face shines upon me and you have always been gracious unto me. I ask you to lift up the light of your countenance upon me and to give me your peace.[1] Thank you for the blessing of your presence, for you never leave me nor forsake me.[2] Thank you for your blessing of peace in my life and for always helping me.[3] Think upon me, O God, for good.[4]

You have prepared a table before me in the presence of my enemies. You have anointed my head with oil, and my cup overflows. Surely goodness and mercy will follow me all the days of my life, and I will dwell in your house forever.[5] Be merciful unto me, Father, and bless me. Cause your face to shine upon me.[6]

89

Thank you for your blessings of wisdom, knowledge, and joy.[7] Blessed be your name forever and ever.[8] Let your peace come upon my house[9] and upon my family.

Lord, I praise and thank you for the gift of your Holy Spirit in my life.[10] He fills me with every spiritual blessing.[11] He guides me into all truth.[12] He comforts me.[13] He brings to my remembrance the things that you have taught me.[14] He gives me the words to speak at times when I feel speechless.[15] He sets my feet to dancing,[16] gives me freedom,[17] quickens my body,[18] and gives me the power to witness to others about your saving grace in my life.[19] I praise you for each of these blessings, and for the certain knowledge that your gifts and your calling do not change.[20] Eye has not seen and ear has not heard the things you have prepared for those who love you.[21] Thank you, Father; you are able to do exceeding abundantly above all that I can ask or think, according to your power that works in me.[22] I praise you that you are at work in me, both to will and to work your good pleasure.[23]

Thank you for your grace[24] that saved me and set me free. As I count my blessings, Lord, I realize how truly and wonderfully blessed I am.

References: *(1) Numbers 6:24-26; (2) Hebrews 13:5; (3) 1 Chronicles 12:18; (4) Nehemiah 5:19; (5) Psalms 23:5-6; (6) Psalms 67:1; (7) Ecclesiastes 2:26; (8) Daniel 2:20; (9) Matthew 10:13; (10) John 20:22; (11) Ephesians 1:3; (12) John 14:17; (13) John 14:26; (14) John 14:26; (15) Ephesians 6:19; (16) Psalms 30:11; (17) 2 Corinthians 3:17; (18) Romans 8:11; (19) Acts 1:8; (20) Romans 11:29; (21) 1 Corinthians 2:9; (22) Ephesians 3:20; (23) Philippians 2:13; (24) Ephesians 6:24.*

Brokenness Before the Lord

Key Thought: God responds to a contrite heart.

Key Scripture: *"The sacrifices of God are a broken spirit, A broken and a contrite heart — These, O God, you will not despise" (Ps. 51:17, NKJV).*

Prayer: Heavenly Father, let my heart be broken with the things that break your heart. Change my heart, Lord, and make me more like you.[1] I humble myself before you, and I thank you for your promise that humility and the reverent fear of the Lord bring riches, honor, and life.[2]

Thank you for your promise that you will be near to those that are of a broken heart. You save those who have a contrite spirit. Though the afflictions of the righteous may be many, you, Lord, will deliver me from all afflictions.[3] Thank you, Lord.

I bow before you, Father, in the full realization that you are the high and lofty One who inhabits eternity. Your name is holy, and you dwell in the high and holy place with all those who are of a humble and contrite spirit. I always want to dwell with you, Father. Thank you for your promise that you will revive the spirits of the humble and the hearts of all who are contrite. Revive my spirit and my heart, Lord, as I humble myself before you.[4]

Mighty Lord, the heaven is your throne and the earth is your footstool. You have made all things. Even though all creation is yours, you have chosen to look upon me when I maintain a humble and contrite spirit before you. I do so now, Lord, and I tremble at your majesty and the power of your glory and your Word.[5]

Thank you for your promise to bind up the broken-hearted.[6] You have promised the very kingdom of heaven to those who are poor in spirit, depending totally upon you, for your Word declares that the poor in spirit are blessed because theirs is the kingdom of heaven.[7] I humble myself under your mighty hand, Father, that you may lift me up in due time.[8]

Lord, you lift up the meek. Therefore, I sing unto you with thanksgiving. I sing praises unto you. You cover the heaven with clouds and prepare rain for the earth. You make grass to grow upon the mountains. You give food to your creatures. You take pleasure in those who revere you. I adore you, Father, and I greatly hope in your mercy. Praise your wonderful name.[9]

References: *(1) 2 Corinthians 3:18; (2) Proverbs 22:4; (3) Psalms 34:18-19; (4) Isaiah 57:15; (5) Isaiah 66:1-2; (6) Isaiah 61:1; (7) Matthew 5:3; (8) 1 Peter 5:6; (9) Psalms 147:6-12.*

Commitment

Key Thought: True commitment forms an inseparable bond.

Key Scripture: *"And now, Israel, what does the Lord your God require of you, but to fear the Lord your God, to walk in all His ways and to love Him, to serve the Lord your God with all your heart and with all your soul, and to keep the commandments of the Lord and His statutes which I command you today for your good?" (Deut. 10:12-13, NKJV).*

Prayer: Lord, I thank you for your Word that reveals your enduring covenant with your people.[1] Help me to see that your covenant is for me and my family. Your commitment to me will never fail; you are my faithful God.[2] Strengthen me, Father, in my ability to remain faithful to the commitment I've made to you. I want to be able to love and serve you with all my heart and all my soul.[3] I am yours, beloved Lord, and I know you are mine.[4] I want my desire to always be in your direction,[5] and I want always to follow you. Keep me from all idolatry, Lord.[6]

Help me to be rooted and grounded in your Word.[7] I always want to be steadfast, unmovable, continually abounding in your work, for I know that my labor will never be in vain when I am living in you.[8] I do not want to be like seeds that wither away because they have no roots.[9]

With the patience you build into me, Lord, I will run the race you have set before me, ever looking to Jesus, who is the Author and Finisher of my faith. For the joy that was set before Him, He endured the cross, despising the shame, and now He is set down at your right hand, Father.[10] He, and so great a cloud of witnesses, are helping me to keep my commitment to you.

Thank you, Lord, for your promise that you will not forsake me nor destroy me nor forget the covenant you have made with your people.[11] Not one word of all your good promises has ever failed.[12] I will always remember your covenant with me,[13] and I will endeavor to obey my part of that covenant by keeping my commitment to you as you have kept your commitment to me.[14] You are my God, and I will ever be your servant.[15] I join myself to you, Lord.[16] I am so grateful, Father, for the covenant you have made with our forefathers and with me.[17]

References: *(1) Psalms 119:1-8; (2) Genesis 17:4; (3) Deuteronomy 10:12; (4) Song of Solomon 6:3; (5) Song of Solomon 7:10: (6) 1 John 5:21; (7) Colossians 2:7; (8) 1 Corinthians 15:58; (9) Matthew 13:6; (10) Hebrews 12:1-2; (11) Deuteronomy 4:31; (12) 1 Kings 8:56; (13) Psalms 11:7; (14) Jeremiah 11:4; (15) Jeremiah 30:22; (16) Jeremiah 50:5; (17) Genesis 17:4.*

Confidence in God

Key Thought: "Prayer moves the arm that moves the world" (James Montgomery).

Key Scripture: *"Therefore do not cast away your confidence, which has great reward. For you have need of endurance, so that after you have done the will of God, you may receive the promise" (Heb. 10:35-36, NKJV).*

Prayer: Lord, I believe in you. I trust in you with all my heart, leaning not to my own understanding. In all my ways I will acknowledge you, and I have confidence that you will direct my paths.[1] Father, your faithfulness in my life is truly awesome. Your mercies are renewed to me each morning. All I have ever needed, your hands have provided for me, and all I will ever need, you will provide for me.[2] As I count my blessings, I realize I can never forget your many benefits in my life.[3]

With you, Lord, all things are possible.[4] You are on my side; therefore, I will not fear what mankind or circumstances can do to me.[5] In you, O Lord, do I put my trust.[6] You alone are my rock and my salvation. You are my sure defense; I shall not be moved.[7] Thank you for fighting my battles with and for me, Lord.[8] Because you are for me, I realize that no one can be against me.[9] I can do all things through you because you strengthen me.[10]

The confidence you impart to me gives me strength.[11] It gives me courage and hope. Thank you for strengthening my heart, Lord.[12] Your righteousness enables me to walk securely.[13] I know you will deliver me from evil and from everything that is potentially harmful in my life.[14] I ask you to quicken your Word to my heart and fill me with your faith.[15] May I be like Abraham and give glory to you, being fully convinced that you are able and willing to do the things you have promised.[16]

Thank you for giving me a spirit of power, love, and a sound mind in exchange for the spirit of fear.[17] I will never be ashamed because I know whom I have believed, and I know you are able to keep all that I have committed unto you.[18] You, Lord, are my helper; I will not fear what man can do unto me.[19]

In every circumstance that comes to me, I will be more than a conqueror through Christ who loves me.[20] I am fully persuaded that neither death nor life nor angels nor principalities nor powers nor things present nor things yet to come will ever be able to separate me from the love you have given unto me through Jesus Christ, my Lord and Savior.[21]

References: *(1) Proverbs 3:5-6; (2) Lamentations 3:23; (3) Psalms 103:2; (4) Matthew 19:26; (5) Psalms 118:6; (6) Psalms 71:1; (7) Psalms 62:6; (8) Nehemiah 4:20; (9) Romans 8:31; (10) Philippians 4:13; (11) Isaiah 30:15; (12) Psalms 31:24; (13) Proverbs 10:9; (14) Daniel 6:16; (15) Acts 6:5; (16) Romans 4:20,21; (17) 2 Timothy 1:7; (18) 2 Timothy 1:12; (19) Hebrews 13:6; (20) Romans 8:37; (21) Romans 8:38-39.*

Consecration

Key Thought: "It does not take great men to do great things; it only takes consecrated men" (Phillips Brooks).

Key Scripture: *"But as He who called you is holy, you also be holy in all your conduct, because it is written, 'Be holy, for I am holy'" (1 Pet. 1:15-16, NKJV).*

Prayer: Holy Father, sanctify me and consecrate me through your Word of truth.[1] I want my life to be totally consecrated to you and to your service, Father, because I realize how important it is for me to be separate from the world. I choose to obey you by never touching things that are unclean, Lord.[2] I present unto you my body as a living sacrifice. I pray that you will find the offering of myself acceptable unto you, because I realize that this is my reasonable service to you.[3] I am determined not to be conformed to this world. Transform me, Lord, and renew my mind so that I will be able to prove what is your good and acceptable and perfect will.[4]

To be able to ascend your hill, Lord, I know I must be totally consecrated unto you — set apart for your service. My hands must be clean and my heart must be pure. Help me to achieve these goals, and keep me from lifting up my soul unto vanity, and purge me from all guile and deceitfulness.[5] Let the love of my heart for you and for others always be without hypocrisy, Master, I pray.[6]

You are so very holy, and the whole earth is full of your glory.[7] I want my life to glorify you at all times, because I realize that you sanctified me even before I was born.[8] You chose me from before the foundations of the world.[9] You have called me to bear much fruit.[10] Thank you for your mercy and your love. Help me to teach your people — both by word and deed — the important distinction that must be made between the holy and the profane.[11] Let my life be holiness unto you, Father.[12] Your wonderful Word makes me clean.[13] It sanctifies me.[14] It is the means of consecration in my life.

Lord, I realize that true consecration requires absolute surrender of my will to yours. Therefore, I follow Jesus' example and surrender my will to you now, saying, "Not my will, but your will be done in me and in my life."[15] I abandon myself to your love and your grace.[16] I surrender, Lord! Strengthen me by your Spirit to walk in obedience to your will.[17]

It is such a privilege for me to be your temple, Lord.[18] Help me to keep your temple holy and consecrated, for I know you have not called me unto uncleanness, but unto holiness.[19] Through unity with you, by the Holy Spirit, I am able to partake of your sanctification.[20] Help me to remember that only you are holy.[21] Lord, I want your holiness to fill my life.

References: *(1) John 17:17; (2) 2 Corinthians 6:17; (3) Romans 12:1; (4) Romans 12:2; (5) Psalms 24:3-4; (6) Romans 12:9; (7) Isaiah 6:3; (8) Jeremiah 1:5; (9) Matthew 25:34; (10) John 15:16; (11) Ezekiel 44:23; (12) Zechariah 14:20; (13) John 15:3; (14) John 17:17; (15) Luke 22:42; (16) 1 Corinthians 1:4; (17) Ephesians 3:16; (18) 1 Corinthians 3:17; (19) 1 Thessalonians 4:7; (20) Hebrews 2:11; (21) Revelation 15:4.*

A Consistent Walk

Key Thought: There are more ups than downs when we walk close to Jesus.

Key Scripture: *"Therefore, my beloved brethren, be steadfast, immovable, always abounding in the work of the Lord, knowing that your labor is not in vain in the Lord"* *(1 Cor. 15:58, NKJV).*

Prayer: Heavenly Father, I know it is not your will for me to be erratic in my Christian walk. I want to be steadfast at all times, walking in the consistency you provide for me. You have warned me that an inconsistent person is like a wave of the sea that is driven with the wind and tossed. Such an individual is double-minded, and he or she is unstable in all his or her ways.[1] Increase my faith, Lord,[2] so that I will never waver in my commitment to you and in my obedience to your Word.

Thank you for your promise that I will be able to hold up my face without shame, and I will be able to remain steadfast, because you have taken away all fear from my life.[3] I ask you, Father, to empower me to be steadfast in my heart, and to let that steadfastness give me power over my will at all times.[4] Keep my hope fervent before you, Lord, even in times of hardship, as I rest in the fact that I know you are with me.[5] Thank you for giving me the grace to partake of the life of Christ by faith. He will ever enable me to hold my confidence steadfast unto the end.[6]

Realizing, Lord, that you never lie, I am able to appropriate the truth of your Word for my life. It gives me a strong consolation because the hope you have set before me is the anchor of my soul in the storms of life. Your Word gives me stability and steadfastness; it is a sure and fast anchor, and it gives me complete assurance that Jesus will ever be the High Priest who makes intercession for me.[7] Let me be like Jesus, Lord; He gave me the example of One who was completely consistent. When He steadfastly set His face to go to Jerusalem, no person and no circumstance could dissuade Him.[8] When He put His hand to the plow, He never looked back.[9] I want to be like Him, Lord.

As I have therefore received Christ Jesus as my Lord, I want to walk consistently in Him and with Him, rooted and built up in Him and established in the faith as I have been taught. Help me always to abound therein with thanksgiving, Father, because I know all your fullness resides in Jesus Christ, my Lord.[10]

References: *(1) James 1:6-8; (2) Luke 17:5; (3) Job 11:15; (4) 1 Corinthians 7:37; (5) 2 Corinthians 1:7; (6) Hebrews 3:14; (7) Hebrews 6:19; (8) Luke 9:51; (9) Luke 9:62; (10) Colossians 2:5-9.*

Courage

Key Thought: God gives us the courage to change the things we can.

Key Scripture: *"Oh, love the Lord, all you His saints! For the Lord preserves the faithful, And fully repays the proud person. Be of good courage, And He shall strengthen your heart, All you who hope in the Lord" (Ps. 31:23-24, NKJV).*

Prayer: Lord, I hope in you. I place my trust in you.[1] Give me courage to be strong.[2] I am fully aware that I need courage of heart in order to face the challenges of my life.[3] Through your courage, I will be able to become swifter than an eagle and stronger than a lion.[4] Thank you for this promise, Father.

Lord, you are the strength of my life. I will fear no one and no thing that might rise against me.[5] I know that no weapon formed against me will ever prosper.[6] Be with me and enable me to become a mighty servant of valor in the same way that you empowered Gideon.[7] When my soul faints within me, I will remember you, O Lord.[8] As a result, I know your strength will be made perfect in my weakness.[9]

I take my stand upon your promises, Father. I will be strong in you and in the power of your might.[10] I will not fear, for I know that it is your good pleasure to give me your kingdom.[11] Knowing that you are with me, I am now able to mock at fear and not be afraid.[12] I will not fear what man can do unto me, because I realize that such fear is a trap.[13]

Fear brings discouragement (a state of having no courage). Encourage me, Lord, as I seek your face and stand upon your Word. Your Word is truth, and you are a mighty buckler to all who trust in you.[14]

Empowered by your Spirit, Lord, I will be strong and courageous. I will not be afraid nor dismayed.[15] I will do all that you have placed within my heart to do, for I know you are with me.[16] I will be of good courage, and I will accomplish your purposes in my life.[17]

Thank you for being with me, Lord, and for fighting for me.[18] I will set myself, stand fast, and trust in you. As I do so, I know you will bring your salvation and deliverance to me.[19]

References: (1) Psalms 7:1; (2) 1 Samuel 4:9; (3) 1 Samuel 17:32; (4) 2 Samuel 1:23;(5) Ezekiel 2:6; (6) Isaiah 54:17; (7) Judges 6:12; (8) Jonah 2:7; (9) 2 Corinthians 12:9; (10) Ephesians 6:10; (11) Luke 12:32; (12) Job 39:22; (13) Proverbs 29:25; (14) 2 Samuel 22:31; (15) 2 Chronicles 32:7; (16) 2 Samuel 7:3; (17) Ezra 10:4; (18) Deuteronomy 1:29-30; (19) Exodus 14:13.

Divine Comfort

Key Thought: "Prayer does not change God, but changes him who prays" (Soren Kierkegaard).

Key Scripture: *"But You, O Lord, are a shield for me, My glory and the One who lifts my head. I cried to the Lord with my voice, And He heard me from His holy hill"* (Ps. 3:3-4, NKJV).

Prayer: Lord God, I thank you for the fact that you have not left me comfortless. You have sent your Spirit to be my ever-present Comforter.[1] I will not fear during this time because I know you are with me, and I know you will bless me.[2] I receive your peace and, in so doing, my heart is no longer troubled. Jesus has imparted His peace to me — a peace that the world cannot give, and circumstances cannot take away.[3] Truly, Father, your peace and your comfort pass all understanding.[4]

In quietness and in confidence I find my peace.[5] You always keep me in perfect peace, Father, as long as I keep my mind focused on you.[6] Even when I walk through the valley of the shadow of death, you are with me. You make me to lie down in green pastures. You lead me beside the still waters, and you restore my soul.[7] It gives me such comfort, joy, and peace, Father, to take hold of your promise that you will be with me even if I pass through the flood waters. The rivers shall not overwhelm me, and I will not be burned by the fires of life.[8] Thank you, Lord, for all the promises of your precious Word.

You are the One who brings comfort to my heart.[9] Your comfort is like a mother's comfort for her little one.[10] You are the Balm in Gilead; you are the physician of my soul.[11] Your Word is truth, Father, and you have told me that those who mourn shall be comforted.[12] I appropriate your comfort into my spirit even now. Thank you for the abiding presence of your Spirit that brings joy and comfort to my heart.[13]

Because your Son, my Lord and Savior Jesus Christ, has already overcome the world,[14] I have no reason for care, anxiety, or fear. Your Word brings comfort to my heart, Lord.

You are the Father of mercies and the God of all comfort.[15] Thank you for hearing my prayer.

References: *(1) John 14:16; (2) John 14:18; (3) John 14:27; (4) Philippians 4:7; (5) Isaiah 30:15; (6) Isaiah 26:3; (7) Psalms 23:2-3; (8) Isaiah 43:2; (9) Isaiah 51:12; (10) Isaiah 66:13; (11) Jeremiah 8:22; (12) Matthew 5:4; (13) John 14:16; (14) John 16:33; (15) 2 Corinthians 1:3.*

El Shaddai
(Almighty God)

Key Thought: God can do anything but fail.

Key Scripture: *"Behold, I am the Lord, the God of all flesh: is there any thing too hard for me?" (Jer. 37:27).*

Prayer: How I praise you and adore you, Father, for your mighty power. Truly, nothing is too hard for you. What you speak, you will bring to pass.[1] You are like a consuming fire.[2] You brought your children out of Egypt with your mighty hand and with your outstretched arm.[3] I thank you that I can personally know the support of your everlasting arms beneath me.[4] You made the sun stand still,[5] you opened the Red Sea,[6] you gave your children manna in the wilderness,[7] and you healed the sick.[8] You have accomplished so many great and mighty things in my life as well.

There is none holy like you, Lord, for there is none besides you, neither is there any rock like our God.[9] You, Lord, are my glory and the lifter of my head.[10] No one is able to stand before you.[11] In your hand there is power and might.[12] No one can truly understand the thunder of your power.[13] You can do everything and anything; no thought is hidden from you.[14] I praise you for being the King of glory. You, Almighty God — El Shaddai — are strong and mighty; you are the Lord who is mighty in battle.[15] I thank you for fighting so many of my battles for me.[16] You have shown me how I can stand still in the midst of difficult times and await your salvation.[17] Praise you, Lord.

Almighty Father, you are more powerful than the noise of many waters. You are greater than the mighty waves of the sea.[18] How great you are!

No one can hold back your hand.[19] The Lord is your name.[20] Father, all things are possible unto you,[21] and I believe you now to move by your power in the following situations that I currently face:_____

_____.

Nothing is impossible with you.[22] You are able to take stones and raise up children unto Abraham.[23] You are able to perform miracles,[24] to heal the broken-hearted,[25] to set the captives free,[26] to heal the sick,[27] to raise the dead,[28] to open the eyes of the blind,[29] and to totally transform my life.[30] Thank you, heavenly Father, for your awesome power. To you be glory and dominion forever and ever.[31]

References: (1) Isaiah 46:11; (2) Deuteronomy 9:3; (3) Deuteronomy 26:8; (4) Deuteronomy 33:27; (5) Joshua 10:13; (6) Psalms 74:13; (7) Deuteronomy 8:3; (8) Mark 1:34; (9) 1 Samuel 2:2; (10) Psalms 3:3; (11) 1 Samuel 6:20; (12) 1 Chronicles 29:12; (13) Job 26:14; (14) Job 42:2; (15) Psalms 24:8; (16) Psalms 24:8; (17) 2 Chronicles 20:17; (18) Psalms 93:4; (19) Daniel 4:35; (20) Amos 9:6; (21) Mark 14:36; (22) Luke 1:37; (23) Luke 3:8; (24) Acts 15:12; (25) Isaiah 61:1; (26) Luke 4:18; (27) Matthew 10:8; (28) Acts 13:30; (29) John 11:37; (30) 2 Corinthians 5:17; (31) 1 Peter 5:11.

Encouraging Myself in God

Key Thought: Encouragement leads to inner courage.

Key Scripture: *"Now David was greatly distressed, for the people spoke of stoning him, because the soul of all the people was grieved, every man for his sons and his daughters. But David strengthened [encouraged] himself in the Lord his God" (1 Sam. 30:6, NKJV).*

Prayer: Heavenly Father, I want to be like David in times of distress by encouraging myself in you. When hard times come, I will not fear; I will stand still and see your salvation and your deliverance come to pass.[1] Lord, lately I've felt discouraged because of _____ _____. In the face of this situation, I determine to rise above the circumstances by seating myself in the heavenly places with Christ Jesus, my Lord.[2] I know you will fight for me, and because of this I can hold my peace during times of difficulty.[3]

You have commanded me not to fear or to be discouraged.[4] I take my stand upon your promises, and I determine not to let this situation get the best of me. Thank you for going before me, Lord, and for fighting for me.[4] You have given me the strength and the power to be strong and courageous,[5] and these qualities I resolve to maintain with the help of your Spirit.

In the face of my present circumstances, I will get up; I will not lie on my face in despair.[6] I will keep on keeping on. I will go up, because I know you will deliver my enemies into my hands.[7] I will be victorious. Praise your name, Father.

I know that as I do all that is in my heart to do, in obedience to your Word, you will be with me.[8] You will never leave me nor forsake me.[9] You will be with me always.[10]

I will persevere with your help, and I will not let my hands be weak, for I know that my work will be rewarded.[11] Keep me from all faint-heartedness, Lord,[12] as I stand strong in you and in the power of your might[13] in order to fight the good fight of faith.[14] I will be strong; I will not fear because I know you will come with vengeance, Lord.[15]

Lord, you are great and you are greatly to be praised in your city, in the mountain of your holiness.[16] You are my God forever and ever. You will be my guide even unto death.[17] I will fear no evil, for you are with me, and you always comfort me and bring encouragement to my heart.[18] Thank you, Lord, for being my glory and the lifter of my head.[19]

References: *(1) Exodus 14:13; (2) Ephesians 2:6; (3) Exodus 14:14; (4) Deuteronomy 1:21; (5) Deuteronomy 31:6; (6) Joshua 7:10; (7) Judges 20:28; (8) 2 Samuel 7:3; (9) Hebrews 13:5; (10) Matthew 28:20; (11) 2 Chronicles 15:7; (12) Isaiah 7:4; (13) Ephesians 6:10; (14) 1 Timothy 6:12; (15) Isaiah 35:4; (16) Psalms 48:1; (17) Psalms 48:14; (18) Psalms 23:4; (19) Psalms 3:3.*

Friendship With Jesus

Key Thought: "What a friend we have in Jesus, all our sins and griefs to bear. What a privilege it is to carry everything to Him in prayer."

Key Scripture: *"No longer do I call you servants; for a servant does not know what his master is doing; but I have called you friends, for all things that I heard from my Father I have made known to you. You did not choose Me, but I chose you and appointed you that you should go and bear fruit, and that your fruit should remain, that whatever you ask the Father in My name He may give you" (John 15:15-18, NKJV).*

Prayer: Heavenly Father, I thank you for the friendship of Jesus. Truly, He is a friend that sticks closer than any brother.[1] He is the same yesterday, today, and forever.[2] He will never fail me.[3] Earthly friends may prove untrue, but I praise you that Jesus never fails.

In the same way that Abraham was known as "a friend of God," I would like others to know that my friendship with Jesus Christ sustains and upholds me at all times.[4] No one has greater love than the love you showed by sending your only begotten Son to be my friend,[5] and the love He demonstrated by laying down His life for His friends.[6]

Teach me how to love Him with all my heart, soul, strength, and mind, and to love my neighbor as myself,[7] for this is the greatest commandment of all. By my love shall all men know that I am a disciple and friend of Jesus Christ, and I want to love fully and completely. Let my love be without hypocrisy, Father.[8] I want always to speak the truth in love.[9]

Thank you for my ongoing friendship with Jesus. He loves me at all times, and like a brother, He is always there to help me in difficult times.[10] My Lord and Savior Jesus Christ is a very present help, a faithful friend, during every difficulty I face.[11]

Thank you for Jesus, Father. I praise you for the peace I have with you through my Lord Jesus.[12] He is the Lamb of God,[13] the Messiah,[14] the Son of man,[15] the Bread of Life,[16] the Light of the world,[17] the door,[18] the Good Shepherd,[19] the way, the truth, and the life,[20] the true vine,[21] the Holy One,[22] the Deliverer,[23] the Judge,[24] the faithful witness,[25] the morning star,[26] the Word of God,[27] the King of kings and Lord of lords,[28] the Alpha and Omega,[29] and He is my faithful friend. It is because of Him that I am able to experience and give love, for He first loved me.[30]

Lord Jesus, I love you and I thank you that you are my Lord and you are also my very best friend.

References: *(1) Proverbs 18:24; (2) Hebrews 13:8; (3) 1 Corinthians 13:8; (4) James 2:23; (5) John 15:13; (6) John 15:13; (7) Matthew 19:19; (8) Romans 12:9; (9) Ephesians 4:15; (10) Proverbs 17:17; (11) Psalms 46:1; (12) Romans 5:1; (13) John 1:29; (14) John 1:41; (15) John 1:51; (16) John 6:35; (17) John 8:12; (18) John 10:9; (19) John 10:11; (20) John 14:6; (21) John 15:1; (22) Acts 3:14; (23) Romans 11:26; (24) James 5:9; (25) Revelation 1:5; (26) Revelation 2:28; (27) Revelation 19:13; (28) Revelation 19:16; (29) Revelation 22:13; (30) 1 John 4:19.*

The Gift of Speech

Key Thought: "O, for a thousand tongues to sing my great Redeemer's praise."

Key Scripture: *"But no man can tame the tongue. It is an unruly evil, full of deadly poison. With it we bless our God and Father, and with it we curse men, who have been made in the similitude of God....Who is wise and understanding among you? Let him show by good conduct that his works are done in the meekness of wisdom" (James 3:8-13, NKJV).*

Prayer: Heavenly Father, thank you for the gift of speech. Help me to use it to glorify you at all times. Put a watch before my lips, O Lord, and keep the door to my mouth. Let my prayer be set before you as incense, and the lifting up of my hands as the evening sacrifice.[1] Help me always to be careful about how I use my speech, Father. Even though my tongue is small, I realize that it can boast great things.[2] Keep me humble, Lord.[3] Help me to use the gift of speech to speak a word in season to those who need encouragement.[4] I choose to walk uprightly before you, not participating in gossip, backbiting, and slander, Lord.[5] I want to walk circumspectly, redeeming the time, because I know the days are evil.[6]

The tongue is a fire, a world of iniquity. It has the power to defile the whole body and it can set the world on fire. Tame my tongue, Lord, so that I would use it only to bless you and your people. May I never use it to curse those you made in your own image.[7]

Father, I never want to take your sacred name in vain, because I love you and I do not want to offend you or grieve your heart.[8] Let my mouth produce blessing and not cursing.[9] Help me to show forth your works in the meekness of wisdom, with conduct pleasing to you, Father.[10]

May no corrupt communication ever proceed from my mouth.[11] Keep me from bitter envying and strife, and help me never to lie against your truth.[12] Let me use the gift of speech to praise you,[13] to speak the truth in love, [14] to encourage others, [15] to bless those who curse me,[16] to forgive those who wrong me,[17] to tell others about your great love,[18] to teach your truth,[19] and to pray without ceasing.[20]

Lord, put your words in my mouth.[21] Keep the door of my lips.[22] Let my speech always be seasoned with grace.[23] Because your lovingkindness is better than life, my lips shall praise you forever.[24]

References: *(1) Psalms 141:2; (2) James 3:5; (3) 2 Corinthians 12:21; (4) Proverbs 15:23; (5) Psalms 15:2-3; (6) Ephesians 5:16; (7) James 3:9; (8) Exodus 20:7; (9) James 3:10; (10) James 3:13; (11) Ephesians 4:29; (12) James 3:14; (13) Psalms 34:1; (14) Ephesians 4:15; (15) 1 Corinthians 14:3; (16) Matthew 5:44; (17) Colossians 3:13; (18) Acts 1:8; (19) 2 Timothy 2:15; (20) 1 Thessalonians 5:17; (21) Jeremiah 1:9; (22) Psalms 141:3; (23) Colossians 4:6; (24) Psalms 63:3.*

God's Guidance

Key Thought: God is the producer and the director of your life.

Key Scripture: *"Your word is a lamp to my feet and a light for my path" (Ps. 119:105, NIV).*

Prayer: Heavenly Father, I thank you for guiding my life and leading me. Show me your way so that I might know your will.[1] I ask you to be my vision, my eyes, my all.[2] You are my lamp, O Lord.[3] You lead me beside the still waters, and you restore my soul.[4] Show me your ways, O Lord. Teach me your paths.[5] You will guide the meek with judgment and you will teach me your ways.[6] You order the steps of a good person, Father, and you delight in the way of a person who is following you.[7] With all my heart, I want to be that person who brings joy and delight to your heart.

Send out your light and truth; let them lead me.[8] You are my God forever and ever; you will be my guide even unto death.[9] Your Word is a lamp unto my feet, and a light unto my path.[10] Cause me to know the way in which I should walk.[11] Attend to my prayer, Father, as I incline my ear to your Word.[12]

Your commandments are a lamp, and your law is light.[13] Give me your counsel so that I might not fall.[14]

Give my your vision so that I will not perish.[15] Let me hear your voice saying unto me, "This is the way, walk in it."[16] Help me to be a light to the people around me,[17] as I walk in your everlasting light, Father.[18] O Lord, correct me with your judgment so that I will be able to adhere ever more closely to your path.[19] When I sit in darkness, I know you will be a light unto me.[20] Guide me with your eye, Father.[21] Let me walk with Jesus who is the Light of the world.[22] He is the way, the truth, and the life, and no one can come unto you, Father, except by going through Him.[23]

Lord, what will you have me to do? Show me your plan and purpose for my life.[24] Help me to fulfill the destiny you have outlined for me. I know you will tell me all that I am to do.[25] Bring to my remembrance all the things that you have taught me,[26] and help me to remember the words of the Lord Jesus.[27] I want your Word to dwell in me.[28] In the light of your Word, Lord, I will be able to make straight paths for my feet at all times.[29] I praise you, Lord, and I love you with all my heart.

References: *(1) Exodus 33:13; (2) Numbers 10:31; (3) 2 Samuel 22:29; (4) Psalms 23:2-3; (5) Psalms 25:4; (6) Psalms 25:9; (7) Psalms 37:23; (8) Psalms 43:3; (9) Psalms 48:14; (10) Psalms 119:105; (11) Psalms 143:8; (12) Proverbs 4:20; (13) Proverbs 6:23; (14) Proverbs 11:14; (15) Proverbs 29:18; (16) Isaiah 30:21; (17) Isaiah 49:6; (18) Isaiah 60:19; (19) Jeremiah 10:24; (20) Micah 7:8; (21) Psalms 32:8; (22) John 8:12; (23) John 14:6; (24) Acts 9:6; (25) Acts 9:6; (26) John 14:26; (27) Acts 20:35; (28) Colossians 3:16; (29) Hebrews 12:13.*

The Goodness of God

Key Thought: "O taste and see that the Lord is good" (Ps. 34:8).

Key Scripture: *"For the Lord is good; His mercy is everlasting; And His truth endures to all generations" (Ps. 100:5, NKJV).*

Prayer: God in heaven, I thank you for your everlasting goodness. You are not a god who takes pleasure in wickedness.[1] Because you are good, I can be sure that goodness and mercy will follow me all the days of my life, and I will dwell in your house forever.[2] The earth is full of your goodness, O Lord.[3]

Thank you for your goodness and your mercy which endure forever.[4] Because of your goodness, you are a stronghold for me in the day of trouble.[5] I cling to you, Father, because I know you are good.

Your goodness leads me to repentance.[6] Because of your goodness to me, I now repent of the following sins:_____
_____. Thank you, Father, for healing me, forgiving me, and restoring me.

I hold fast to you because you are good.[7] I resolve to do good with your help, Lord.[8] How I thank you for every good and perfect gift that I have received from your goodness, Father.[9]

I believe to see your goodness revealed in the land of the living, as I wait on you. I resolve to be of good courage, Lord, and I know you will strengthen my heart.[10] Praise your name forever. Oh, how great is your goodness which you have laid up for them that revere you.[11] Your goodness endures continually, Father.[12]

Oh, that people everywhere would praise you for your goodness, and for your wonderful works to us.[13] Lord, you are my strength, my goodness, my high tower, and my deliverer. I trust in you with all my heart,[14] for you have been so good to me.

I praise you, Father, for the riches of your goodness, your forbearance, and your longsuffering.[15] I resolve in my heart to continue always in your goodness.[16] I pray, Lord, that you would count me worthy of your calling. I beseech you to fulfill all the good pleasure of your goodness and the work of faith with power so that the name of my Lord Jesus Christ, your Son, will be glorified in my life, according to your grace.[17]

References: *(1) Psalms 5:4; (2) Psalms 23:6; (3) Psalms 33:5; (4) Psalms 106:1; (5) Nahum 1:7; (6) Romans 2:4; (7) 1 Thessalonians 5:21; (8) 1 Timothy 6:18; (9) James 1:17; (10) Psalms 27:13; (11) Psalms 31:19; (12) Psalms 52:1; (13) Psalms 107:8; (14) Psalms 144:2; (15) Romans 2:4; (16) Romans 11:22; (17) 2 Thessalonians 1:11-12.*

A Heart for Worship

Key Thought: True worship is loving God.

Key Scripture: *"You shall love the Lord your God with all your heart, with all your soul, and with all your strength" (Deut. 6:5, NKJV).*

Prayer: Lord, I want to learn how to worship you in spirit and in truth, for I know you seek people with a pure heart to worship you.[1] You are my God, and I will prepare a place in my heart for you. You are my God, and I will exalt you.[2] With all my heart and soul I want to serve you, honor you, and worship you.[3] Help me to keep my hands clean, my heart pure, and to prevent my heart from being lifted up to vanity so that I will be able to ascend your hill and stand in your holy place.[4]

Father, you are worthy to receive honor, glory, and love from your people.[5] You are high and lifted up, and your train fills the Temple.[6] When you commanded me to seek your face, my heart responded that I will seek your face at all times.[7] To me, Lord, your lovingkindness is better than life.[8]

I kneel before you because I know you are my Maker.[9] I give unto you the glory that is due your name.[10] I desire to worship you fully, in the beauty of holiness,[11] and I always want to seek you, your strength, and your face.[12] With my soul have I desired you in the night, and with my spirit I will seek you early.[13]

I bow my knee to you, Father, because I know the time will come when every knee will bow before you and every tongue will confess you.[14] Praise your holy name. You are the only one I want to serve, Lord.[15]

Thank you for the direct access I have to you through your Son, my Lord and Savior Jesus Christ.[16] Because of Him, I am able to come into your presence with thanksgiving, to enter your courts with praise.[17] I thank you, Lord, that I am able to know your voice, and I thank you that you know your sheep.[18] Speak to me now as I worship you and behold your glory.[19]

You are worthy of all honor, glory, and majesty because you have created all things.[20] In you all things consist.[21] You are the God in whom I live and move and have my being.[22] There is no one like you, O Lord.[23] You were before all things,[24] and in you all things consist and have their being.[25] I bow before you and I worship you, because you are Almighty God, you are my Father, you are the God who loves me, and I love you.

References: *(1) John 4:24; (2) Exodus 15:2; (3) Deuteronomy 6:5; (4) Psalms 24:3,4; (5) Revelation 4:11; (6) Isaiah 6:1; (7) Psalms 105:4; (8) Psalms 63:3; (9) Psalms 95:6; (10) Psalms 96:8; (11) 1 Chronicles 16:29; (12) Psalms 105:4; (13) Isaiah 26:9; (14) Romans 14:11; (15) Matthew 4:10; (16) 1 Timothy 2:5; (17) Psalms 100:4; (18) John 10:27; (19) Isaiah 40:5; (20) Revelation 4:11; (21) Colossians 1:17; (22) Acts 17:28; (23) Psalms 136:4; (24) Colossians 1:17; (25) Colossians 1:17.*

Holy Boldness

Key Thought: Boldness stems from confidence.

Key Scripture: *"According to his eternal purpose which he accomplished in Christ Jesus our Lord. In him and through faith in him we may approach God with freedom and confidence"* *(Eph. 3:11-12, NIV).*

Prayer: Heavenly Father, I come boldly before your throne of grace because I know that in your presence I will obtain mercy and find grace to help in my time of need.[1] Lord, I need greater boldness and confidence in my praying, witnessing, and living. Thank you for hearing my prayer. This is the confidence I have in you: when I ask anything according to your will, I know you hear me, and I know you will give me the petitions I request of you as long as they are in accord with your will and your Word.[2]

Show me how to become as bold as a lion in all aspects of my life.[3] Help me to open my mouth boldly so that I might make known the mystery of your gospel to others.[4] I am not ashamed of your gospel, Lord, because I know it is your power unto salvation to all those who will believe.[5] I want to speak boldly in your behalf[6] as I hold forth the Word of life to those who do not know you.[7]

Thank you for the divine empowerment that comes through the impartation of your Spirit in my life. Fill me with Him, Lord, so that I will always be your witness everywhere I go.[8] As Peter and John sought for greater boldness to preach your Word, Lord, I come to you now, asking you to give me the boldness to stand firm, to expose the works of darkness,[9] to not be afraid of other people,[10] to speak the truth in love,[11] to assault the kingdom of darkness, and to share your truth with others.[12]

My earnest expectation and my hope are based on your Word, Lord. This is what imparts boldness and confidence to my spirit. Because of the spiritual resources you have given to me, I know that I will never be ashamed in anything, but will, with all boldness, let Christ be magnified in my body, whether by life or by death.[13] Praise His holy name!

For to me to live is Christ, and to die is gain.[14] Thank you for giving me great boldness in the faith which is in Christ Jesus.[15] In Him my love is made perfect and, therefore, I have boldness to face the day of judgment,[16] not in my own strength, but because of Him who loved me and gave himself for me.[17] Thank you, Lord.

References: *(1) Hebrews 4:16; (2) 1 John 5:14-15; (3) Proverbs 28:1; (4) Ephesians 6:19; (5) Romans 1:16; (6) Ephesians 6:20; (7) Philippians 2:16; (8) Acts 1:8; (9) Romans 13:12; (10) Proverbs 29:25; (11) Ephesians 4:15; (12) Ephesians 4:25; (13) Philippians 1:20; (14) Philippians 1:21; (15) 1 Timothy 3:13; (16) 1 John 4:17; (17) Galatians 2:20.*

Hospitality

Key Thought: Hospitality is an art.

Key Scripture: *"For I was hungry and you gave Me food; I was thirsty and you gave Me drink; I was a stranger, and you took Me in: I was naked and you clothed Me; I was sick and you visited Me; I was in prison, and you came to Me....Assuredly, I say to you, inasmuch as you did it to one of the least of these My brethren, you did it to Me" (Matt. 25:35-36, 40, NKJV).*

Prayer: Heavenly Father, your love has flooded my heart by your Spirit.[1] Help me to share your love with all others you bring to me. Let me truly love others because I know that love is of you and everyone who loves is born of you and knows you. A person who does not love does not know you because you are love.[2]

Help me to remember to treat strangers with hospitality, remembering that your people were strangers in the land of Egypt.[3] Help me to treat visitors in my home as if they were members of my own family, feeding them and caring for them with love and concern.[4] May your peace come upon my family and fill my home at all times.[5]

I believe your promise, Father, that he who receives a prophet in the name of a prophet shall receive a prophet's reward.[6] It is my desire to show hospitality to those servants of your kingdom who visit in my area and home. I thank you for your promise that he who receives a righteous man in the name of a righteous man will receive a righteous man's reward.[7]

Lead me to people who would benefit from my hospitality, Father. Bring them to me. I always want to be ready to give a cup of water in your name because I belong to you.[8] I always want to remember that when I treat another person with hospitality, I am actually ministering to you.[9]

I want to receive whomsoever you send to me in the same way that I would receive your Son, my Lord and Savior, Jesus Christ.[10] Help me never to be forgetful to entertain strangers, for by so doing, some have entertained angels unawares.[11] What a privilege that would be for me, Father — to entertain one of your angel-messengers.

It is my desire, Lord, to treat my brothers and sisters in Christ with respect, honor, and love at all times. Teach me how to use hospitality in my relationships with fellow-believers, and may I always do so without grudging.[12] Give my your wisdom in all the situations of my life, because I know that wisdom is the foundation of hospitality, the home, and the hearth.[13]

References: *(1) Romans 5:5; (2) 1 John 4:7-8; (3) Exodus 22:21; (4) 1 Samuel 28:22; (5) Matthew 10:13; (6) Matthew 10:41; (7) Matthew 10:41; (8) Mark 9:41; (9) Matthew 25:40; (10) John 13:20; (11) Hebrews 13:2; (12) 1 Peter 4:9; (13) Proverbs 4:7.*

Humility

Key Thought: "It was pride that changed angels into devils; it is humility that makes men as angels" (St. Augustine).

Key Scripture: *"Take my yoke upon you and learn from me, for I am gentle and humble in heart, and you will find rest for you souls" (Matt. 11:29, NIV).*

Prayer: Dear Lord, without you I can do nothing.[1] You are the Potter; I am the clay.[2] Mold me and shape me according to your will.[3] I want to obey you in all things, Lord, to do justly, to love mercy, and to walk humbly with you.[4]

You have promised to save the humble person,[5] and you preserve the simple.[6] Help me to keep my life simple and my attitude humble. I thank you for your promise that honor will be given to those who are humble.[7] Keep leading me into all humility, I pray, so that I can experience the blessedness you promise to those who are poor in spirit. It is exciting for me to realize that the humble are heirs of the Kingdom of heaven.[8] You have also promised, Lord, that the meek will inherit the earth.[9] Keep me meek and humble, I pray.

Your gracious invitation to come unto you when I am weary and heavy-laden gives rest to my soul. I can take your yoke upon me because I know your yoke is easy and your burden is light. Thank you for the example of Jesus who was meek and lowly in heart;[10] help me to be like Him.

You have promised to exalt those who humble themselves,[11] and it is my prayer that I would learn how to humble myself so that I would always walk in humility. The one who is least among us will be considered great;[12] Lord, through humility, I want to be pleasing to you at all times. Your Son, my Lord Jesus Christ, came to serve others.[13] He stated that even He could do nothing of himself.[14] I want His mind to be my mind,[15] and His attitude of service and humility to fill my heart. My sufficiency is of you, Father.[16]

Your strength is made perfect in my weakness.[17] You resist the proud, but you give grace to the humble.[18] Prove your strength to me, Father, and give me your grace to keep a meek and humble spirit. Clothe me with humility.[19] I now recognize that it is by humility and the reverential fear of you that riches, honor, and life are imparted to me.[20] Thank you, Lord, for your grace in my life.

References: *(1) John 15:5; (2) Isaiah 64:8; (3) Romans 8:29; (4) Micah 6:8; (5) Job 22:29; (6) Psalms 116:6; (7) Proverbs 15:33; (8) Matthew 5:3; (9) Psalms 37:11; (10) Matthew 11:29; (11) Luke 14:11; (12) Luke 9:48; (13) Luke 22:27; (14) John 5:30; (15) Philippians 2:5; (16) 2 Corinthians 3:5; (17) 2 Corinthians 12:9; (18) James 4:6; (19) 1 Peter 5:5; (20) Proverbs 22:4.*

Increasing Faith

Key Thought: God is pleased by your faith.

Key Scripture: *"We ought always to thank God for you, brothers, and rightly so, because your faith is growing more amd more, and the love every one of you has for each other is increasing" (2 Thess. 1:3, NIV).*

Prayer: Faithful Father, I come to you in faith and expectancy concerning all that you will accomplish in my life and in the lives of those I love. You will never fail me, forsake me, or leave me, and because I believe your promises, I know I will never be dismayed.[1] Increase my faith, Lord,[2] as I meditate upon your Word.[3]

You are the Lord who delivered David out of the paws of the lion and the paws of the bear, and I know you will deliver me during times of difficulty as well.[4] Help me always to remember that the battle is yours, not mine, O Lord.[5] You are my lamp,[6] and by believing in you, I know my life will be established.[7] I want to trust in you at all times.[8]

As I pour my heart out to you, Father, I realize more and more that you are my strong refuge.[9] Whom have I in heaven but you?[10] The just shall live by faith, Father,[11] and I want to be so full of faith that I will be able to live victoriously at all times. I know that as I believe your Word, so will it be done unto me.[12] My faith will make me whole.[13]

Through the faith you give, nothing shall be impossible unto me.[14] Thank you for your precious gift of faith, Father; help me to nurture it, cultivate it, and develop it through the reading and appropriating of your Word.[15]

You have shown me that the perfect antidote for fear is faith.[16] Fill me with faith, Lord. I want never to be afraid, but only to believe.[17] All things are possible to the person who believes,[18] and I want to be a true believer — a person who lives in the realm of the infinite possibilities that come by way of faith in you, in your Word, and in your truth. It is truly wonderful to know that when I pray a believing prayer, I will receive directly from you.[19] Teach me to pray in faith, nothing wavering, at all times.[20] Impart to me greater understanding of the righteousness that comes through faith, Lord.[21] Help me to always remember that whatsoever is not of faith is sin.[22]

Grant unto me your sustaining power so that I will always stand fast in the faith,[23] walking by faith and not by sight,[24] having nothing and yet possessing all things.[25] By grace I was saved through faith,[26] and I know that it is faith that will keep me as well. I resolve to take up the shield of faith whereby I will be able to quench all the fiery darts of the wicked one.[27]

References: *(1) Deuteronomy 31:8; (2) Luke 17:5; (3) Psalms 1:2; (4) 1 Samuel 17:37; (5) 1 Samuel 17:47; (6) 2 Samuel 22:29; (7) 2 Chronicles 20:20; (8) Psalms 62:8; (9) Psalms 71:7; (10) Psalms 73:25; (11) Romans 1:17; (12) Matthew 8:13; (13) Mark 5:34; (14) Matthew 17:20; (15) Romans 10:17; (16) Mark 5:36; (17) Matthew 8:26; (18) Mark 9:23; (19) Mark 11:24; (20) James 1:6; (21) Romans 4:13; (22) Romans 14:23; (23) 1 Corinthians 16:13; (24) 2 Corinthians 5:7; (25) 2 Corinthians 6:10; (26) Ephesians 2:8; (27) Ephesians 6:16.*

Inner Abundance

Key Thought: The kingdom of heaven is within you!

Key Scripture: *"You, dear children, are from God and have overcome them, because the one who is in you is greater than the one who is in the world"* (1 John 4:4, NIV).

Prayer: Dear Lord, I thank you that you have chosen to take up residence in my heart. When I heard you knocking at the door of my heart, I opened it, and you came into me, and it has been my life's greatest joy to sup with you ever since.[1] Keep on filling me with your Spirit, Lord, so that I can experience the inner abundance you promise to all who love you, and so that I can share it with others.[2] My body is the temple of your Spirit, because you bought me with blood of Jesus Christ, my Lord. Therefore, I am no longer my own; I am yours and you are my God.[3] Have your way in my life at all times, Father, and lead me in the paths that please you.[4]

Fill me with all your fullness, Father, so that I will be able to draw upon your spiritual resources, the wells of life, that bubble within my spirit.[5] Strengthen me with all might in my inner being.[6] I invite Christ to always dwell in my heart by faith so that I would be rooted and grounded in love.[7] I want to be able to comprehend with all saints the breadth and length and depth and height of your love which passes knowledge, O Lord, and be filled with all of your fullness.

Teach me to be spiritually minded, Father, because I realize that to be carnally minded is death, but to be spiritually minded is life and peace.[8] Lord, I greatly desire to be filled with your life and peace. Thank you for filling up the empty places in my heart and life and replacing them with your abundance. Even though my outward man is perishing, I know that my inner man is being renewed day by day.[9] Thank you, Father, for the riches of your Spirit that I find deep within my heart.

Your kingdom is so much more than meat and drink; it is righteousness, peace, and joy in your Holy Spirit.[10] It thrills me when I realize that you live within me by your Spirit, and because this is true, your righteousness, peace, and joy strengthen me and flow forth from my life to others.[11]

References: *(1) Revelation 3:20; (2) Ephesians 5:18; (3) 1 Corinthians 3:16; (4) Psalms 27:11; (5) Ephesians 3:19; (6) Ephesians 3:16; (7) Ephesians 3:17; (8) Romans 8:6; (9) 2 Corinthians 4:16; (10) Romans 14:17; (11) Luke 17:21.*

Inspiration

Key Thought: The breath of God inspires us.

Key Scripture: *"The word that God puts in my mouth, that I must speak"* (Num. 22:38, NKJV).

Prayer: Heavenly Father, I thank you for the inspiration of your Spirit that enables me to speak forth in your behalf,[1] to hear your voice,[2] to discern your will,[3] and to proclaim your goodness.[4] Thank you for always being with me, and even for being with my mouth and for teaching me what I should say.[5] I will boldly proclaim your Word as you inspire me.[6] Thank you for the Scriptures, Lord, the holy words that you have given to us through the inspiration of your Holy Spirit. Those words are always profitable to me in the areas of righteousness, doctrine, correction, understanding, and instruction.[7] I praise you for your Word.

When your Spirit inspired Gideon, he was able to blow the trumpet and the walls of Jericho came tumbling down.[8] Samuel prophesied to Saul that your Spirit would inspire him.[9] Through inspiration, your Spirit is able to speak through me,[10] and I invite Him to do so at all times.

Rest your hand upon me, Lord.[11] Pour out your Spirit upon me.[12] When I speak in your behalf to others, I pray that the words will not be mine, but rather the words of your Spirit speaking through me.[13] I realize so fully, Lord, that a person can receive nothing unless it comes from your hands.[14] Truly, without you, I can do nothing,[15] but through you, I can do all things.[16]

You have redeemed me, Lord, and I want to let others know what you have done in my life.[17] You have lifted me from the miry clay and set me on the solid rock of your Word.[18] I take my stand upon your Word, Father. Help me to write the things which I have seen, and the things that are, as well as the things that shall be hereafter through the inspiration of your Spirit.[19]

The anointing I have received from you abides within me. The precious anointing of your Spirit in my life teaches me all things,[20] and guides me into all truth.[21] Thank you for your promise that assures me that if I will abide in Jesus and let His words abide in me, I will be able to ask whatever I will and it shall be done.[22] Thank you, Lord.

References: (1) Ephesians 6:19-20; (2) John 10:27; (3) 1 Peter 2:15; (4) Psalms 145:7; (5) Exodus 4:12; (6) Numbers 22:38; (7) 2 Timothy 3:16; (8) Judges 6:34; (9) 1 Samuel 10:6; (10) 2 Samuel 23:2; (11) Ezekiel 37:1; (12) Joel 2:28; (13) Matthew 10:20; (14) John 3:27; (15) John 15:5; (16) Philippians 4:13; (17) Psalms 107:2; (18) Psalms 40:2; (19) Revelation 1:19; (20) 1 John 2:27; (21) John 16:13; (22) John 15:7.

Intimacy With God

Key Thought: "There is a place of quiet rest near to the heart of God."

Key Scripture: *"Draw near to God and He will draw near to you" (James 4:8, NKJV).*

Prayer: Heavenly Father, how I praise you for your faithfulness to me which is new every morning.[1] You are a very present help to me.[2] Thank you for sending your Son, my Lord and Savior Jesus Christ, who is the way, the truth, and the life.[3] Through Him, I am able to have fellowship with you, Father, and His shed blood enables me to have access to your throne of glory.[4] I come before your throne with confidence, knowing that you hear me and that you will always provide grace and mercy in my times of need.[5]

Lord, you have made it possible for me to be more than your servant. It amazes me to realize that you have called me to be your friend.[6] The closer I get to you, the more you open my understanding to your wonderful ways and to your truth.[7] Draw me ever closer, Father, and I will run after you.[8]

You have brought me to your banqueting table, and your banner over me is love.[9] You have anointed my head with the oil of your Holy Spirit.[10] You are my Beloved and I am yours; you feed me among the lilies and you supply my every need.[11] I am so happy to be a part of your bride, Lord, and I ask you to continue your workmanship in my life and the lives of all your followers so that we will be spotless and without blemish.[12]

Set me as a seal upon your heart, O Lord, as a seal upon your strong arm. Your love is stronger than death.[13] Nothing shall be able to separate me from your great love.[14] Many waters cannot quench your love; neither can the floods drown it.[15] I want to give back a portion of all that you have given to me, O beloved One. I realize that to whom much has been given, much shall be required.[16] Teach me to love you with all my heart, soul, mind, and strength.[17] I want you to have the preeminence in all that I say, think, and do.[18] Greater love has no one than the love that was demonstrated by Jesus who willingly laid down His precious life for us. Thank you, Father, for your overwhelming love which leads me to love you because you first loved me.[19]

Draw me nearer, heavenly Father. It is my deepest desire to ever dwell in the midst of your love and the intimacy of your presence.

References: *(1) Lamentations 3:23; (2) Psalms 46:1; (3) John 14:6; (4) Ephesians 2:13; (5) Hebrews 4:16; (6) John 15:14; (7) Psalms 119:18; (8) Song of Solomon 1:4; (9) Song of Solomon 2:4; (10) Psalms 23:5; (11) Song of Solomon 6:3; (12) Ephesians 5:27; (13) Song of Solomon 8:6; (14)Romans 8:36-39; (15) Song of Solomon 8:7; (16) Luke 12:48; (17) Mark 12:30; (18) Colossians 1:18; (19) 1 John 4:19.*

Jehovah-Elohim
(The Lord Who Is Worthy of Worship)

Key Thought: "It is only when men begin to worship that they begin to grow" (Calvin Coolidge).

Key Scripture: *"Who may ascend into the hill of the Lord? Or who may stand in His holy place? He who has clean hands and a pure heart, Who has not lifted up his soul to an idol, nor who has sworn deceitfully. He shall receive blessing from the Lord, And righteousness from the God of his salvation" (Ps. 24:3-5, NKJV).*

Prayer: Dear Lord, you alone are worthy of my worship, honor, reverence, and devotion; all things were created for your pleasure.[1] I want to bring pleasure to your heart, Father, to see you as the sovereign and majestic Lord of the universe who is always worthy of worship. You are Jehovah-Elohim, and I adore you.

You are my God, and I will prepare a habitation for you within my heart and I will exalt you.[2] I want to love you with all my heart, soul, mind, and strength.[3] I want to learn how to worship you in spirit and in truth.[4] Lead me in these important areas of my life, Lord.

You have told me to seek your face, and my heart is responding unto you. I will seek your face at all times, Lord.[5] I will give you glory and strength.[6] I will give you the glory that is due to your name.[7] Teach me to worship you in the beauty of holiness,[8] to bow down in your presence, fully realizing that you are the Lord, my Maker.[9]

With my soul have I desired you in the night; my spirit leads me to seek you early each morning.[10] I know that when I seek you, I will be found of you.[11] Thank you, Father, for the precious promises of your Word. As I draw near to you, you draw near to me.[12] I thank you for your presence that cheers and guides me at all times.[13]

I will worship you, Father, for who you are, and for all you have done for me. I will serve you alone.[14] When I cry unto you, I know you will hear me.[15] You are near unto all who call upon you, to those who call upon you in truth.[16] I call upon you now, Father, and I ask you to guide me into all truth.[17]

Blessed be your name. You have heard the voice of my supplication.[18] Unto you, O Lord, do I lift up my soul,[19] and I thank you that you are a rewarder of those who diligently seek you.[20]

References: *(1) Revelation 4:11; (2) Exodus 15:2; (3) Matthew 22:37; (4) John 4:24; (5) Psalms 27:8; (6) Psalms 29:1; (7) 1 Chronicles 16:29; (8) Psalms 96:9; (9) Psalms 95:6; (10) Isaiah 26:9; (11) 1 Chronicles 16:11; (12) James 4:8; (13) John 16:13; (14) Matthew 4:10; (15) Psalms 34:17; (16) Psalms 145:18; (17) John 16:13; (18) Psalms 28:6; (19) Psalms 25:1; (20) Hebrews 11:6.*

Jehovah-Elyon
(The Lord God Most High)

Key Thought: Jesus is the King of kings and the Lord of lords.

Key Scripture: *"Yours, O Lord, is the greatness, The power and the glory, The victory and the majesty; For all that is in heaven and in earth is Yours. Yours is the kingdom, O Lord, And You are exalted as head over all. Both riches and honor come from You, And You reign over all. In Your hand is power and might; In Your hand it is to make great And to give strength to all. Now therefore, our God, We thank You, And praise Your glorious name"* (1 Chron. 29:11-13, NKJV).

Prayer: Heavenly Father, how I praise, honor, and adore you for who you are — Jehovah-Elyon, the Lord God Most High. The kingdom is yours.[1] You are the King of all the universe; therefore, I sing unto you praises with spiritual understanding.[2] Justice and judgment are the habitation of your throne. Mercy and truth go before your face.[3] Almighty God, you reign forever and, because of this, the earth rejoices.[4] I rejoice in you, heavenly Father.[5] I will rejoice evermore in the knowledge of your greatness.[6]

You, O Lord, remain forever.[7] You are the Alpha and Omega — the beginning and the end.[8] Your throne will remain from generation to generation.[9] Of your kingdom there shall be no end.[10] No one is like you, Lord.[11] You are high and lifted up, and your train fills the Temple.[12] Heaven is your throne, and the earth is your footstool.[13] The earth is yours, and the fullness thereof.[14] You have created all things for your pleasure.[15]

By your Son, my Lord and Savior Jesus Christ, all things were created that are in heaven and on earth, both those things that are visible and those that are invisible. He has created thrones, dominions, principalities, powers, and all things were created by Him and for Him. He is before all things, and by Him all things hold together. Jesus is the Head of the Body — your Church — He is the beginning, the firstborn from the dead. I want Him to have the preem-inence in every aspect of my life, Father, for it pleased you that in Him all fullness should dwell. He made peace through the blood of His cross, thereby reconciling all things unto himself.[16] Thank you for Jesus, Father. I look forward to the day when every knee shall bow and every tongue will confess that Jesus Christ is Lord to your eternal glory.[17]

You will reign until all your enemies have been put under your feet.[18] Hasten that day, Father. How I praise you that your throne, O God, is forever and ever.[19]

References: *(1) 1 Chronicles 29:11; (2) Psalms 47:7; (3) Psalms 89:14; (4) Psalms 97:1; (5) Philippians 4:4; (6) Psalms 47:7; (7) Lamentations 5:19; (8) Revelation 1:8; (9) Lamentation 5:19; (10) Luke 1:33; (11) Micah 7:18; (12) Isaiah 6:1; (13) Acts 7:49; (14) 1 Corinthians 10:26,28; (15) Revelation 4:11; (16) Colossians 1:16-20; (17) Romans 14:11; (18) 1 Corinthians 15:25; (19) Hebrews 1:8.*

Jehovah-Jireh
(God, My Provider)

Key Thought: "Providence knows what we need better than we ourselves" (Jean de La Fontaine).

Key Scripture: *"And my God shall supply all your need according to His riches in glory by Christ Jesus. Now to our God and Father be glory forever and ever. Amen"* *(Phil. 4:19-20, NKJV).*

Prayer: Father, you know what things I have need of before I even express them to you.[1] I come to you today with the certain knowledge that you know I need the following:_____
_____. It is my heart's desire to seek you and your righteousness first, and as I do so, I know you will meet every need of my life.[2] Thank you, Lord, for all the precious promises of your glorious Word.

You will never forsake the righteous, and none of us shall ever have to beg for bread.[3] You are the Bread of life,[4] and everyone who hungers and thirsts after you shall be filled.[5] I am thirsty for the water of life that you provide so freely.[6] Freely I have received so much from your hands; therefore, I want to give to others freely as well.[7] Help me to be generous with all you have given to me, Lord.

You are the Giver of every good and perfect gift, the Father of lights with whom there is no variation nor shadow of turning.[8] Thank you for all the gifts you have bestowed upon me. Heavenly Father, how I praise you for your promise to give good things to those who ask you.[9] Everyone who asks, your Word declares, will receive.[10]

Help me to learn to obey you and serve you at all times so that I will be able to enjoy your blessings in this life and in the life to come.[11] You will bring all the good you have promised upon your people.[12] You will supply my daily bread.[13] You are my Shepherd; I shall not want. You make me to lie down in green pastures; you lead me beside the still waters. You restore my soul. You lead me in the paths of righteousness for your name's sake. Yea, though I walk through the valley of the shadow of death, I will fear no evil: for you are with me. Your rod and your staff bring comfort to me. You prepare a table before me in the presence of my enemies; you anoint my head with oil, and my cup overflows. Surely goodness and mercy shall follow me all the days of my life, and I will dwell in your house forever.[14]

Thank you, Lord, for being my Jehovah-Jireh, the One who supplies every need of my life — physically, emotionally, and spiritually. You can do anything but fail! Hallelujah!

References: *(1) Matthew 6:8; (2) Matthew 6:33; (3) Psalms 37:25; (4) John 6:35; (5) Revelation 22:17; (6) Matthew 5:6; (7) Matthew 10:8; (8) James 1:17; (9) Matthew 7:11; (10) Luke 11:10; (11) Job 36:11; (12) Jeremiah 32:42; (13) Luke 11:3; (14) Psalms 23.*

Jehovah-m'Kaddesh
(God Who Sanctifies)

Key Thought: God chose you!

Key Scripture: *"Who may ascend into the hill of the Lord? Or who may stand in His holy place? He who has clean hands and a pure heart, Who has not lifted up his soul to an idol, Nor sworn deceitfully. He shall receive blessing from the Lord, And righteousness from the God of his salvation" (Ps. 24:3-5, NKJV).*

Prayer: Heavenly Father, I thank you for the assurance I have that when I confess my sins, you will forgive me and you will cleanse me from all unrighteousness.[1] Wash me in the water of your Word.[2] Purify my heart so that I will be able to see you.[3] Wash me, and I shall be whiter than snow.[4]

Help me to be careful to use the gift of speech properly, for I know it is not what goes into my mouth that defiles me, but those things that proceed from my mouth can defile me.[5] I never want to engage in lying, gossip, bragging, slander, cursing, or harmful criticism. Instead, Lord, I want to be clean through the Word you have spoken to me.[6]

Thank you for choosing me to be the temple of your Holy Spirit. I want to keep your temple clean, pure, and undefiled, because I know that your temple must be kept holy at all times.[7] I want to glorify you both in my body

and in my spirit.[8] You have not called me unto uncleanness, Father, but you have called me unto holiness.[9] I want
to be holy in the same way you are holy.[10] Sanctify me as
I endeavor to keep myself pure.[11]

Give me the strength, Lord, to flee youthful lusts that war
against my soul.[12] Keep me from all double-mindedness,
because the double-minded person is unstable in all his
ways.[13] I will cleanse my hands and purify my heart in obedience to your Word.[14] Sanctify me through your truth, Lord.[15]

I reach out and take hold of your hand. From his time
forward, I will walk in your Spirit; by so doing, I know I
will not fulfill the lusts of the flesh.[16] I will live in your
Spirit.[17] Continually fill me with your Spirit, Lord.[18]

I thank you that your Spirit dwells within me.[19] Let
the fruit of your Spirit be manifested in all my relationships
and responsibilities today. I choose to walk in love, peace,
joy, patience, meekness, gentleness, faithfulness, goodness,
and self-control, through the power of your Spirit.[20] As I do
so, Father-God, I know that you are sanctifying (purifying,
setting me apart for service, consecrating) me for the work
you have for me to do. I love you, Lord God, for you are
Jehovah-m'Kaddesh, the God of my sanctification.

References: *(1) 1 John 1:9; (2) John 15:3; (3) Matthew 5:8; (4) Psalms
51:7; (5) Matthew 15:11; (6) John 15:3; (7) 1 Corinthians 3:17;
(8) 1 Corinthians 6:20; (9) 1 Thessalonians 4:7; (10) 1 Peter 1:16;
(11) Leviticus 22:2; (12) 2 Timothy 2:22; (13) James 1:8; (14) James
4:8; (15) John 17:17; (16) Galatians 5:16; (17) Galatians 5:25;
(18) Ephesians 5:18; (19) 1 Corinthians 3:16; (20) Galatians 5:22-23.*

Jehovah-Nissi
(God, the Conqueror)

Key Thought: Faith is the victory that overcomes the world.

Key Scripture: *"Your right hand, O Lord, has become glorious in power; Your right hand, O Lord, has dashed the enemy in pieces. And in the greatness of Your excellence You have overthrown those who rose against You; You sent forth Your wrath; it consumed them like stubble"* *(Exod. 15:6-7, NKJV).*

Prayer: Almighty God, Jehovah-Nissi, you are the God of battles.[1] Victory is already yours.[2] How I thank you that I am more than a conqueror through your mighty power.[3] The devil is already a defeated foe.[4] All power in heaven and in earth is yours, Lord.[5]

I will sing unto you because you have triumphed gloriously. You have thrown the horse and his rider into the sea.[6] You have overthrown those who have risen against you. You send forth your wrath and consume your enemies as if they are stubble.[7] Because this is true, I know that no weapon formed against me shall prosper.[8] Thank you, Father, for making me strong in you and in the power of your might.[9]

Help me always to remember that I do not fight against flesh and blood, but against spiritual entities that

influence regions, people, and institutions.[10] Through you, however, I shall be able to chase my enemies and they will fall.[11] You will save me from my enemies — whether they be people, demonic powers, or circumstances. Lord, I ask you now to save and deliver me from:_____
_____. Thank you for the victory that you have already won for me in this area of my life.

Lord God, thank you for fighting for me.[12] My strength is increased over my enemies because I rejoice in your salvation.[13] I know that you love me, Lord, because my enemies cannot triumph over me.[14]

This is the day which you have made, and I will rejoice and be glad in it.[15] I am happy because you have overcome the world.[16] You give me complete victory through Jesus Christ, my Lord.[17] Because I am born of you, I can overcome the world, too, through the power of your Spirit.[18] As I do so, you will give me hidden manna to eat — your spiritual provisions that enable me to endure.[19] Through the blood of Jesus and the word of my testimony, I will overcome,[20] for Jesus is the Lord of lords and the King of kings.[21] Alleluia! You, the Lord God omnipotent, reign forever! As I overcome through you, Father, I know I shall inherit all things.[22] Praise your mighty name.

References: *(1) Psalms 24:8; (2) 1 Chronicles 29:11; (3) Romans 8:37; (4) Colossians 2:15; (5) Matthew 28:18; (6) Exodus 15:1; (7) Exodus 15:7; (8) Isaiah 54:17; (9) Ephesians 6:10; (10) Ephesians 6:12; (11) Leviticus 26:7; (12) Joshua 10:14; (13) 1 Samuel 2:1; (14) Psalms 41:11; (15) Psalms 118:24; (16) John 16:33; (17) 1 Corinthians 15:57; (18) 1 John 5:4; (19) Revelation 2:17; (20) Revelation 12:11; (21) Revelation 17:14; (22) Revelation 21:7.*

Jehovah-Olam
(My Everlasting God)

Key Thought: "God is a light that is never darkened; an unwearied life that cannot die; a fountain always flowing; a garden of life; a seminary of wisdom; a radical beginning of all goodness" (Francis Quarles).

Key Scripture: *"But the Lord is the true God; He is the living God and the everlasting King. At His wrath the earth will tremble, And the nations will not be able to endure His indignation....He has made the earth by His power, He has established the world by His wisdom, And has stretched out the heavens at His discretion" (Jer. 10:10-12, NKJV).*

Prayer: Everlasting King — Jehovah-Olam — it is such a pleasure for me to be your servant. You are my praise.[1] You are my life and the length of my days.[2] You are the Rock, and your work is perfect.[3] I know that you are greater than all gods.[4] There is none like you, and there is no God besides you.[5] You are exceedingly great, your power and your understanding are infinite.[6]

Your mercy is great unto the heavens and your truth unto the clouds.[7] Your lovingkindness is better than life to me.[8] Your mercy endures forever.[9] You are full of compassion; you are gracious, longsuffering, and plenteous in mercy and truth.[10] I thank you that all your wonderful attributes are everlasting.[11] You are a God who is ever ready to pardon your people.[12] Praise you, Lord.

Nothing is too hard for you.[13] All things are possible with you.[14] You, O Lord, are a shield for me; you are my glory and the lifter of my head.[15] You are my sure defense.[16] Your name is a strong tower into which I can always run and find safety.[17] You are my keeper.[18] You never slumber or sleep.[19] My help is in your name, dear Father.[20]

You are always faithful. You will establish me and you will keep me from evil.[21] You will never fail me nor forsake me.[22] You always fight for me.[23] You are always with me.[24] You are my God. You strengthen me and help me. You always uphold me with the right hand of your righteousness.[25] Truly, you will reign forever and ever.[26] I thank you that you are the living God.[27]

You are my Father, my God, and the Rock of my salvation.[28] Blessed be your name from this time forth and forevermore.[29] You are my Savior and my Redeemer.[30] You are the true God, and all who forsake you will be ashamed.[31] You are the fountain of living waters.[32] Your foundations stand sure.[33] You are light,[34] and you are love.[35] Holy, holy, holy, Lord God Almighty, you always have been, you are now, and you always will be.[36] You are Jehovah-Olam, my everlasting God; you love me and I love you.

References: *(1) Deuteronomy 10:21; (2) Deuteronomy 30:20; (3) Deuteronomy 32:4; (4) Exodus 18:11; (5) 2 Samuel 7:22; (6) Psalms 147:5; (7) Psalms 57:10; (8) Psalms 63:3; (9) Psalms 118:1; (10) Psalms 86:15; (11) Psalms 100:5; (12) Nehemiah 9:17; (13) Genesis 18:14; (14) Mark 14:36; (15) Psalms 3:3; (16) Psalms 59:17; (17) Proverbs 18:10; (18) Psalms 121:5; (19) Psalms 121:3; (20) Psalms 124:8; (21) 2 Thessalonians 3:3; (22) Deuteronomy 31:6; (23) Nehemiah 4:20; (24) Joshua 3:10; (25) Isaiah 41:10; (26) Exodus 15:18; (27) Psalms 18:46; (28) Psalms 89:26; (29) Psalms 113:2; (30) Isaiah 60:16; (31) Jeremiah 10:10; (32) Jeremiah 17:13; (33) 2 Timothy 2:19; (34) 1 John 1:5; (35) 1 John 4:8; (36) Revelation 4:8.*

Jehovah-Repheka
(God, My Healer)

Key Thought: "God heals, and the doctor takes the fee" (Benjamin Franklin).

Key Scripture: *"'For I will restore health to you And heal you of your wounds,' says the Lord" (Jer. 30:17, NKJV).*

Prayer: Almighty God, Jehovah-Repheka, you are my healer, the Great Physician of my soul and body. You are the Lord who heals me.[1] Thank you for the provisions of health and healing you have revealed in your Word.

You want me to be blessed, Father. Above all else, you want me to prosper and to be in health, even as my soul prospers.[2] Thank you for restoring my soul,[3] and for giving me a merry heart that is like a good medicine to me.[4] As you bless me spiritually, my soul prospers and my body enjoys good health. Lord, I ask you to bless my health in the following ways: _____
_____. How I praise you that you say in your Word: "Therefore I tell you, whatever you ask for in prayer, believe that you have received it, and it will be yours."[5] Help me, Lord, to believe that I receive your provisions when I pray.

The leaves of the tree of life are for the healing of the nations;[6] you forgive my iniquities and you heal all my diseases.[7] I honor you, heavenly Father; when I cry to you, you heal me.[8] You heal the broken in heart and you bind up the wounds of those who love you.[9] With your stripes I am healed.[10] Your promise to those who love you and revere your name is that the Sun of righteousness shall arise with healing in His wings.[11] Help me to remember that precious promise, Lord, whenever illness threatens, and give me boldness to declare that your promise of healing is true.[12]

You are the Balm in Gilead, the heavenly Physician.[13] Heal me, O Lord, and I shall be healed; save me, and I shall be saved.[14] Help me to realize the important relationship between faith and healing. As Jesus revealed, it is my faith that makes me whole.[15] His touch makes a person completely whole.[16] He enables the deaf to hear, the blind to see, the mute to speak, and He has the power to heal every disease.[17] He makes me whole,[18] and His Spirit within me gives life and health to my mortal body.[19]

Father, I thank you for the fact that the prayer of faith does save the sick, and you are able and willing to raise up one who is ill.[20] I pray the prayer of faith now for the following people who are enduring affliction in their lives:_____
_____.

References: (1) Exodus 15:26; (2) 3 John 2; (3) Psalms 23:3; (4) Proverbs 17:22; (5) Mark 11:24; (6) Revelation 22:2; (7) Psalms 103:3; (8) Psalms 30:2; (9) Psalms 147:3; (10) Isaiah 53:5; (11) Malachi 4:2; (12) Acts 4:29; (13) Jeremiah 8:22; (14) Jeremiah 17:14; (15) Matthew 9:22; (16) Matthew 14:36; (17) Mark 7:37; (18) Matthew 9:21; (19) Romans 8:11; (20) James 5:15.

Jehovah-Ro'eh
(The Lord Is My Shepherd)

Key Thought: "He leadeth me; O blessed thought!"

Key Scripture: *"For this God is our God for ever and ever: he will be our guide even unto death" (Ps. 47:14).*

Prayer: Lord, you are my Shepherd. I shall not want. You make me to lie down in green pastures. You lead me beside the still waters. You restore my soul. You lead me in the paths of righteousness for your name's sake. Yea, though I walk through the valley of the shadow of death, I will fear no evil because I know you are with me. Your rod and your staff comfort me. You prepare a table before me in the presence of my enemies. You anoint my head with oil. My cup overflows. Surely goodness and mercy shall follow me all the days of my life, and I will dwell in your house forever.[1] Hallelujah!

You have always been the guide and shepherd of your people, Lord, and I ask you to guide and shepherd me.[2] You are the Good Shepherd of your sheep.[3] Thank you that I am a sheep in your flock, Lord — one who knows your voice. Help me to hear your voice clearly. How I thank you that you know each of your sheep personally,[4] and you love each one. You love us so much, in fact, that you will leave the sheepfold in order to find one of your flock that gets lost.[5] I pray that you will show me your way. I desire to hear your voice saying to me, "This is the way, walk in it."[6]

I will attend to your words, and incline my ear to your sayings.[7] Impart your vision to me, Lord, and help me to embrace it, run with it, and see it come into reality. Where there is no vision, Master, the people perish.[8] I want to live in accord with the vision you impart to me.

Show me your ways, O Lord. Teach me your paths.[9] Your Word is a lamp unto my feet and a light unto my path.[10] Send out your light and your truth; let them lead me.[11] Cause me to know the way in which I should walk.[12] Your commandment is a lamp, and your law is a light.[13] You are the Light of the world, and unto me you are an everlasting light.[14] I will walk in the light of your Word and in your love.

As I let your Word dwell in me,[15] I will remember the words of my Lord Jesus,[16] I will stand solidly on the realization that He is the way, the truth, and the life,[17] and I will make straight paths for my feet.[18] By these means, therefore, I know that my God — Jehovah-Ro'eh — will ever be my Shepherd. Thank you, Father, for all your promises to me.

References: *(1) Psalms 23; (2) Exodus 13:21; (3) John 10:11; (4) John 10:27; (5) Luke 15:6; (6) Isaiah 30:21; (7) Proverbs 4:20; (8) Proverbs 29:18; (9) Psalms 25:4; (10) Psalms 119:105; (11) Psalms 43:3; (12) Psalms 143:8; (13) Proverbs 6:23; (14) John 8:12; (15) Colossians 3:16; (16) Acts 20:35; (17) John 14:6; (18) Hebrews 12:13.*

Jehovah-Shalom
(God, My Peace)

Key Thought: "Speak, move, act in peace, as if you were in prayer. In truth, this is prayer" (Francois de Salignac de La Mothe Fenelon).

Key Scripture: *"You will keep him in perfect peace, Whose mind is stayed on You, Because he trusts in You" (Isa. 26:3, NKJV).*

Prayer: Jehovah-Shalom, you are my Father and you are my peace. Thank you for giving me the peace which surpasses all understanding.[1] Your Son, my Lord and Savior Jesus Christ, has imparted His peace to my heart. Therefore, my heart is not troubled because I believe in Him. His peace far exceeds anything the world has to offer, and I am so thankful for it.[2]

Lord, I realize that carnal-mindedness leads to death and confusion.[3] You are not the author of confusion, but you are the author of peace.[4] Help me to remember the importance of being spiritually minded, for this is the source of true and lasting peace and life.[5] One name of Jesus, my Lord, is the Prince of Peace,[6] and with Him dwelling within my heart, I am able to enjoy His peace. I will let the peace of Christ rule in my heart so that I will always know the right path.[7]

I want all my ways to please you, Lord, because I know that when my ways please you, you make even my enemies to be at peace with me.[8] So fill me with your peace that I will be able to live peaceably with all people.[9] Let your peace rest upon my home,[10] and let peace reign on earth so that people will glorify you as Lord and will live in goodwill toward each other.[11]

Peace-making leads to happiness and blessedness; Lord, make me a peacemaker in your kingdom.[12] Thank you for blessing your people with peace.[13] A righteous person always ends his or her life in peace.[14] Great peace have they who love your law, and nothing shall be able to offend them.[15] You want peace to rule within the walls of my home, and you want me and my family to experience prosperity.[16] Thank you, Father.

I choose to walk in quietness and in confidence because I know these two sources of peace of mind will give me strength.[17] How beautiful upon the mountains are the feet of those who bring good tidings and those who publish peace.[18] As I put your peace upon my feet,[19] Lord, help me to be a faithful messenger of your peace and truth.

I pray for peace in the following areas of my life: _____,and I pray for the following people who need your blessing of peace at this time in their lives: _____
_____.

References: *(1) Philippians 4:7; (2) John 14:27; (3) Romans 8:6; (4) 1 Corinthians 14:33; (5) Romans 8:6; (6) Isaiah 9:6; (7) Colossians 3:15; (8) Proverbs 16:7; (9) Romans 12:18; (10) Luke 10:5; (11) Luke 2:14; (12) Matthew 5:9; (13) Psalms 29:11;(14) Psalms 37:37; (15)Psalms 119:165; (16) Psalms 122:7; (17) Isaiah 30:15; (18) Isaiah 52:7; (19) Ephesians 6:15.*

Jehovah-Shammah
(The God Who Is There)

Key Thought: The Lord is only a prayer away.

Key Scripture: *"The Lord is near to all them who call upon Him, To all who call upon Him in truth. He will fulfill the desire of those who fear Him: He also will hear their cry and save them. The Lord preserves all who love Him"* *(Ps. 145:18-20, NKJV).*

Prayer: Thank you for always being there for me, Lord. When I call unto you, you always answer me.[1] O my God, incline your ear and hear me.[2] Let the words of my mouth and the meditations of my heart be acceptable in your sight, O Lord, my strength and my Redeemer.[3] Be not far from me in times of trouble. I need you and I know you are my only true help.[4] You are a Friend who sticks closer than a brother.[5]

Unto you, O Lord, I lift up my soul.[6] I bless you, because I know you hear all my supplications.[7] Father, I ask you now to intervene in the following areas of my life:_____.
Thank you for always being a very present help to me.[8]

When I seek you, you hear me and you deliver me from all my fears.[9] O Lord, keep not silence; be not far from me.[10] O Lord, hear. O Lord, forgive. O Lord, hearken and do.[11] Thank you for being rich unto all who call upon you.[12]

You will never leave me nor forsake me.[13] You are with me always, even unto the end of the age.[14] You are the same yesterday, today, and forever.[15] You never change.[16] You are always there. By prayer and supplication, with thanksgiving, I am able to let my requests be made known unto you.[17] Your eyes behold me, and your ears are open unto my prayers.[18]

Whatsoever I ask in prayer, believing, I shall receive.[19] Thank you, Father, for granting my requests. Let your Word so fill my heart with faith[20] that when I ask, I shall receive, and through this wonderful promise I will experience fullness of joy.[21] I will extol you, my God, O King, and I will bless your name forever and ever. Every day will I bless you, and I will praise your name forever and ever. You are so great and you are greatly to be praised. Your greatness is unsearchable.[22]

Lord, you are gracious and full of compassion. You are slow to anger and you are of great mercy. You are good to all, and your tender mercies are over all your works.[23] You are Jehovah-Shammah, my God who is always there for me. Thank you for your abiding presence in my life.

References: *(1) Psalms 4:3; (2) Daniel 9:18; (3) Psalms 19:14; (4) Psalms 35:22; (5) Proverbs 18:24; (6) Psalms 25:1; (7) Psalms 28:6; (8) Psalms 46:1; (9) Psalms 34:4; (10) Psalms 35:22; (11) Daniel 9:19; (12) Romans 10:12; (13) Hebrews 13:5; (14) Matthew 28:10; (15) Hebrews 13:8; (16) Malachi 3:6; (17) Philippians 4:6; (18) 1 Peter 3:12; (19) Matthew 21:22; (20) Romans 10:17; (21) John 16:24; (22) Psalms 145:1-3; (23) Psalms 145:8-9.*

Jehovah-Tsidkenu
(God, My Righteousness)

Key Thought: Righteousness is a gift from God.

Key Scripture: *"Blessed are they which do hunger and thirst after righteousness: for they shall be filled" (Matt. 5:6).*

Prayer: Lord, you are my righteousness; you are Jehovah-Tsidkenu — the Holy One — and I come to you with a heart full of thanksgiving because you have enabled me to partake of your righteousness through faith in Jesus Christ.[1] All have sinned and fallen short of your glory,[2] and no one is able to do good apart from you.[3] Because I know this is true, I recognize my constant need for you. Without you, I can do nothing good.[4] Through you, however, I can do all things,[5] I can be a fruitful believer,[6] and I can be holy because you are holy.[7] Thank you, Father.

You never forsake the one you make righteous, Lord.[8] You have promised to reward the righteous.[9] Help me to remember at all times the strong relationship between faith and righteousness; as your Word points out, Lord, Abraham believed you and it was counted unto him as righteousness.[10]

In the same way that mercy and truth go together, righteousness and peace kiss each other.[11] Thank you for the gift of righteousness that gives me peace. Those who are planted in the house of the Lord shall flourish in the courts of our God.[12] Through your righteousness, Lord, I can flourish spiritually and be bold as a lion.[13]

I put on your breastplate of righteousness, Father, and I know it will protect me, along with the shield of faith, from all the fiery darts of the enemy.[14] Lord, I always want to do that which is right in your sight.[15] Empower me to fulfill righteousness at all times. You lead me in the paths of righteousness for your name's sake.[16] Your eyes are upon me, and your ears are open to my cries.[17] The righteous shall inherit the land,[18] and there is a true reward for the righteous.[19] You love those who are righteous, Father.[20] Thank you for your love.

The fruit of the righteous is a tree of life,[21] and in the house of the righteous there is much treasure.[22] Thank you for the wonderful gift of righteousness.

References: *(1) Romans 3:22; (2) Romans 3:23; (3) Psalms 14:3; (4) John 15:5; (5) Philippians 4:13; (6) John 15:5; (7) 1 Peter 1:16; (8) Psalms 37:25; (9) Psalms 58:11; (10) James 2:23; (11) Psalms 85:10; (12) Psalms 92:12; (13) Proverbs 28:1; (14) Isaiah 59:17; (15) 2 Kings 14:3; (16) Psalms 23:3; (17) Psalms 34:15; (18) Psalms 37:29; (19) Psalms 58:11; (20) Psalms 146:8; (21) Proverbs 11:30; (22) Proverbs 15:6.*

Knowing and Doing God's Will

Key Thought: God's will is revealed in His Word.

Key Scripture: *"I delight to do Your will, O my God, And Your law is within my heart" (Ps. 40:8, NKJV).*

Prayer: O my God, thank you for revealing your will to me through your Word. I hide it in my heart so that I might not sin against you.[1] I delight to do your will,[2] and I ask you to reveal your will to me in every area of my life.

You are the Lord of the universe, and you are my Lord; therefore, I ask you to do whatever seems to be good to you in my life.[3] Your way is perfect in all things.[4]

My Father in heaven, your name is holy. Let your kingdom come, and let your will be done on earth as it is in heaven.[5] I surrender to you, Lord. Not my will, but yours, be done at all times.[6] Let your will be done in my life, Father.[7]

Realizing that the world will one day pass away, with all its lusts, I fully recognize that the one thing that truly counts is that I should endeavor to accomplish your will. Thank you for your promise that the person who does your will shall live forever.[8] I praise you for this certainty, Father.

Help me to build my life upon the certainty of your promises, Lord. What you have spoken you will bring to pass.[9] Your Word is quick and powerful and sharper than any two-edged sword.[10] Help me to wield the sword of your Spirit, which is the Word of God, in all my battles with the enemy.[11] I thank you, Father, that the weapons of spiritual warfare are not carnal, but they are mighty through your Holy Spirit.[12]

I know that it is not your will that any should perish, but that all should come to a knowledge of eternal life.[13] Thank you for sending Jesus, Father, and help me to be His ambassador at all times.[14]

Show me how to be a faithful prayer warrior, Lord, for I know it is your will for me to rejoice evermore, to pray without ceasing, and to give thanks in everything through Christ Jesus.[15]

Help me to be like Jesus who said that His sustenance and nourishment came from doing your will at all times.[16] Your Word is a light unto my path and a lamp unto my feet, revealing your will for me each step of the way.[17] Lead me by your Spirit,[18] and help me to walk in the light of your Word and your perfect will at all times, following in the footsteps of my Lord Jesus Christ.[19]

References: (1) Psalms 119:11; (2) Psalms 40:8; (3) 1 Samuel 3:18; (4) Psalms 18:30; (5) Matthew 6:9-10; (6) Luke 22:42; (7) Acts 21:14; (8) 1 John 2:17; (9) Isaiah 46:11; (10) Hebrews 4:12; (11) Ephesians 6:17; (12) 2 Corinthians 10:4; (13) 2 Peter 3:9; (14) Ephesians 6:20; (15) 1 Thessalonians 5:16-18; (16) John 4:34; (17) Psalms 119:105; (18) Romans 8:14; (19) 1 Peter 2:21.

Love for God

Key Thought: God is love.

Key Scripture: *"You shall love the Lord your God with all your heart, with all your soul, and with all your mind. This is the first and great commandment" (Matt. 22:37-38, NKJV).*

Prayer: Dear heavenly Father, thank you for the gift of love that led me to Jesus in the first place.[1] I want to love you more fully and more deeply.[2] As the deer pants after the brooks of water, so does my heart pant after you, O Lord.[3] My soul thirsts for you like a thirsty land seeks water.[4]

How I praise you and thank you, Father, for your glorious promise that all things will work together for good to those who love you.[5] Nothing shall be able to separate me from your love.[6] The human eye has not seen and the human ear has not heard all the things you hold in store for those who love you.[7] Thank you, Lord.

Always keep me in the center of your love as I look for the mercy of my Lord Jesus Christ.[8] He loves me and gave himself for me.[9] I am complete in Him who is the head of all principality and power.[10] At His name, every knee shall bow and every tongue shall confess that He is Lord.[11] He is before all things, and by Him all things consist.[12] When I realize all that Jesus is to me, my heart is overcome with love and adoration for you, Father, and for Him.

Thank you for the Great Commandment that was given to us by Jesus, Father, that we should love one another.[13] I pray that the love you have poured into my heart by your Holy Spirit will have great effect in me to walk in love at all times.[14]

I love you, Lord, because you first loved me.[15] You gave your Son to die for me, and there can be no greater love than this.[16] I draw near to you now, and as I do so, I know you are drawing near to me.[17] I want to have an intimate relationship with you, Lord, so that I will always dwell near your heart. I want to be one with you as you and Jesus are one.[18] Your love is so much better than anything in life.[19] Thank you for choosing me as your beloved.[20]

References: *(1) John 3:16; (2) Deuteronomy 10:12; (3) Psalms 42:1; (4) Psalms 143:6; (5) Romans 8:28; (6) Romans 8:35; (7) 1 Corinthians 2:9; (8) Jude 21; (9) Galatians 2:20; (10) Colossians 2:10; (11) Philippians 2:10; (12) Colossians 1:17; (13) John 13:34; (14) Romans 5:5; (15) 1 John 4:19; (16) John 15:13; (17) James 4:8; (18) John 17:11; (19) Psalms 63:3; (20) Song of Solomon 2:16.*

A Love for God's Word

Key Thought: "God's Word will keep you from sin, but sin will keep you from God's Word" (Anonymous).

Key Scripture: *"The grass withers, And its flower falls away, But the word of the Lord endures forever"* (1 Pet. 1:24-25, NKJV).

Prayer: Thank you for your sacred Word, Father. In your Word do I hope.[1] It is a lamp unto my feet and a light unto my path.[2] Give me a growing hunger for the Bible at all times, Lord, for I know that if I hunger and thirst after your righteousness, I shall be filled.[3]

Your Word is near to me; it is even in my mouth and in my heart. Thank you for your word of faith that enables me to confess with my mouth the Lord Jesus and to believe in my heart that you have raised Him from the dead. Because of the faith imparted by your Word to my heart, I have been saved.[4] Thank you, Father, for so great a salvation.[5]

Faith comes from the hearing of your Word.[6] Help me to study to show myself approved unto you, a workman who never needs to be ashamed because I rightly divide your Word.[7] Help me to be like the Bereans who searched the Scriptures daily.[8]

Your Word is the sword of your Spirit;[9] it is the greatest weapon I have available to me as I fight the good fight of faith.[10] Let me wield the weapon of your Word strongly as I proclaim your truth with boldness,[11] and thereby defeat every temptation that comes my way as Jesus did in the wilderness.[12]

Your Word is like a fire, O Lord. It is like a hammer that breaks a rock in pieces.[13] Thank you for the power of your Word. It keeps me from sin.[14] It enables me to pray with conviction because I realize that when I abide in you, and let your words abide in me, I will be able to ask whatever I will and it shall be done.[15] That's because, when I let your Word dwell in me, it becomes quick and powerful and sharper than any two-edged sword.[16] Through your Word, Lord, my ways become more like your ways and my thoughts become more like your thoughts because your Word renews my mind.[17]

Your Word is truth.[18] I love and honor your Word because it helps me to know you better; as a newborn babe, I desire the sincere milk of your Word so that I would grow in you.[19] Your Word is so good;[20] it imparts life to my spirit.[21]

References: *(1) Psalms 130:5; (2) Psalms 119:105; (3) Matthew 5:6; (4) Romans 10:8-9; (5) Hebrews 2:3; (6) Romans 10:17; (7) 2 Timothy 2:15; (8) Acts 17:11; (9) Ephesians 6:17; (10) 1 Timothy 6:12; (11) Ephesians 6:19; (12) Matthew 4; (13) Jeremiah 23:29; (14) Psalms 119:11; (15) John 15:7; (16) Hebrews 4:12; (17) Ephesians 5:26; (18) John 17:17; (19) 1 Peter 2:2; (20) 2 Kings 20:19; (21) 1 John 1:1.*

New Beginnings
(A Prayer for Spiritual Renewal)

Key Thought: "Christianity is the land of beginning again" (W.A. Criswell).

Key Scripture: *"Therefore if any man be in Christ, he is a new creature: old things are passed away; behold, all things are become new" (2 Cor. 5:17).*

Prayer: Lord, I thank you that I can always begin anew with you. Jesus has promised that all those who come to Him, He will in no wise cast out.[1] I come to you now, Lord, fully realizing my need for spiritual renewal, my need to begin over again. How wonderful it is to know that you do, in fact, make all things new.[2]

Restore my soul, Father.[3] Renew my strength as I wait on you.[4] I join myself to you and to your purposes for my life.[5] Turn me unto you, O Lord, and I know I shall be turned. Renew my days as of old.[6] I have failed in many important respects, but I know your grace is sufficient for me,[7] your strength is made perfect in my weakness,[8] and your goodness leads me to repentance.[9] I do repent of my sins, Father, in the following areas of my life: _____,
and I ask you to restore me to fellowship with you.

Give me a heart of flesh in place of any hardness of heart.[10] I will enter your rest through obedience, an open heart, and faith in you.[11] Renew me in the spirit of my mind[12] as I return to your Word which is quick and powerful, and sharper than any two-edged sword.[13] Lord, I was like a sheep that wandered far away, but now I am returning to you.[14] You are my Shepherd, and I shall not want.[15] You are the Good Shepherd of the sheep.[16]

I determine to put on the new man in my life every single day from this point forward,[17] to be clothed in righteousness,[18] to seek you with all my heart, soul, mind, and strength,[19] and to give you the preeminence in all that I say, think, and do.[20] Thank you for your all-sufficient grace that makes this possible in my life, Lord.[21] I love you, and I know you first loved me.[22]

As Christ was raised up by your glory, Father, even so I rise to walk in newness of life.[23] Thank you for the power of your resurrection that enables me to begin anew.

References: *(1) John 6:37; (2) Revelation 21:5; (3) Psalms 23:3; (4) Isaiah 40:31; (5) Jeremiah 50:5: (6) Lamentations 5:21; (7) 2 Corinthians 12:9; (8) 2 Corinthians 12:9; (9) Romans 2:4; (10) Ezekiel 11:19; (11) Hebrews 3-4; (12) Ephesians 4:23; (13) Hebrews 4:12; (14) 1 Peter 2:25; (15) Psalms 23:1; (16) John 10:11; (17) Ephesians 4:24; (18) Psalms 132:9; (19) Luke 10:27; (20) Colossians 1:18; (21) 2 Corinthians 12:9; (22) 1 John 4:19; (23) Romans 6:4.*

A New Home

Key Thought: There is no place like home.

Key Scripture: *"Unless the Lord builds the house, They labor in vain who build it; Unless the Lord guards the city, The watchman stays awake in vain" (Ps. 127:1, NKJV).*

Prayer: Dear Lord, thank you for providing me/us with this new home. Watch over it and keep it safe. I ask you to protect all those who dwell within my/our home. Plant your hedge of protection around me/us,[1] and let your angels stand guard in my/our behalf.[2]

Let the foundations of this home be strongly laid,[3] and let your hospitality and your faithful Word be experienced here at all times.[4] Give me/us wisdom[5] so that my/our home will always be secure. Help me/us always to remember that through wisdom a house is built, and by understanding it is established.[6] Thank you for your Word that imparts wisdom and understanding to my/our spirit(s). Truly, it is a lamp unto my/our feet and a light unto my/our path(s).[7]

Father, you are the one who builds all things.[8] I pray that you will build this home and family so that they will endure and remain strong throughout all generations.

Help me/us always to be like the man which built his house on a rock so that when the winds and floods of life

163

swirl about this home, nothing will be able to shake it because it is founded upon the rock of faith in your precious Word.[9] Thank you, Lord, for supplying all my/our needs so faithfully according to your riches in glory by Christ Jesus.[10] I trust in you with all my heart, and I purpose not to lean unto my own understanding. In all my ways, I will acknowledge you as Lord, and I know you will direct my paths.[11]

Let your peace rule within the walls of this home at all times, Lord.[12] I ask that your Son, our Lord and Savior Jesus Christ, would have the preeminence here, in all that is said and done.[13] Teach us your ways, Father, and help us to walk in your paths.[14] As for me and my house, we will serve you, Lord.[15]

Father, I declare that Jesus Christ is the Lord over this home.[16] May all who enter the doors of this home know that your presence is here to cheer and to bless and to guide me/us. May this knowledge lead people to taste and see that you are good.[17]

Lord, you are so great, and you are greatly to be praised.[18] From the rising of the sun to the going down of the same, I will praise you.[19] Morning, noon, and night I will praise you,[20] for your name is wonderful.[21] Thank you for your great faithfulness to us.[22]

References: *(1) Job 1:10; (2) Matthew 4:6; (3) Ezra 6:3; (4) Titus 1:8-9; (5) James 1:5; (6) Proverbs 24:3; (7) Psalms 119:105; (8) Hebrews 3:4; (9) Matthew 7:24-25; (10) Philippians 4:19; (11) Proverbs 3:5-6; (12) Colossians 3:15; (13) Colossians 1:18; (14) Psalms 25:4; (15) Joshua 24:15; (16) Philippians 2:10; (17) Psalms 34:8; (18) Psalms 48:1; (19) Psalms 113:3; (20) Psalms 55:17; (21) Isaiah 9:6; (22) Lamentations 3:23.*

Nutrition and Exercise

Key Thought: Healthy habits lead to healthful living.

Key Scripture: *"Beloved, I pray that you may prosper in all things and be in health, just as your soul prospers"* *(3 John 2, NKJV).*

Prayer: Heavenly Father, thank you for your Word that shows the steps to health and healing for my body, soul, and spirit. When I cry out to you, you bring health to me;[1] help me now to maintain my health by taking good care of my body that was bought by the blood of my Lord and Savior Jesus Christ.[2] I realize that my body is the temple of your Holy Spirit and, therefore, I want to honor you with the way I treat your temple.[3] I want to profit through bodily exercise[4] and good nutrition so that I will be able to serve you more fully.

A merry heart does good like a medicine, Father,[5] and I thank you that you have given me so many reasons to be merry, joyful, and happy. Help me to keep my focus on those things at all times — to think only on things that are honest, true, just, pure, lovely, and of good report.[6] Let me apply your positive principles of health — mental, emotional, and physical — to my daily life.

Help me to walk in the Spirit, Father, so that I might be able to bear the fruit of your Spirit in all my responsibilities and relationships — love, peace, joy, patience, meekness, gentleness, goodness, faithfulness, and self-control.[7] May the fruit of self-control be my daily portion as I endeavor to practice positive principles of good health in my diet and physical exercise. I praise you for your promise to restore health to me,[8] and I ask you to guide me in how to walk in the health you provide for me. Truly, Lord, your joy is my strength,[9] and your Word is life to me.[10]

Thank you, Father, for giving me every herb, and every tree with its fruit, for my nourishment and health.[11] Thank you for the blessing of healthful food. Give me wisdom to govern my eating and exercise habits, and help me make wise choices daily.[12]

References: *(1) Psalms 30:2; (2) 1 Corinthians 6:20; (3) 1 Corinthians 6:19; (4) 1 Timothy 4:8; (5) Proverbs 17:22; (6) Philippians 4:8; (7) Galatians 5:22-23; (8) Jeremiah 30:17; (9) Nehemiah 8:10; (10) 1 John 1:1; (11) Genesis 1:29 (12) James 1:5.*

Patience

Key Thought: Patience — one of the greatest of all virtues.

Key Scripture: *"But let patience have its perfect work, that you may be perfect and complete, lacking nothing" (James 1:4, NKJV).*

Prayer: Father, I know I need patience in order to face the challenges of my daily life. Thank you for providing patience for me through the power of your Spirit.[1] I realize that when my faith is tested I need to let patience have its perfect work in me so that I may be perfect and complete, not lacking anything.[2] I want to learn how to wait on you, Lord.[3] Your way is perfect and your Word is tried.[4] My soul waits for you because you are my help and my shield.[5]

My soul waits for you more than they that watch for the morning, O Lord.[6] Teach me to be slow to wrath and to be one who possesses great understanding.[7] Help me always to remember that the patient in spirit are better than the proud in spirit.[8] Because of your greatness, your glory, and your power, O God, I know that I can wait for you and you will save me, because you are the Lord of all.[9]

Thank you for all the precious promises of your Word, Father. Though the promise may tarry, I will wait for it because I know it will surely come.[10] Your Word is always true, and your faithfulness is unto all generations.[11]

When tribulation comes, help me always to remember that the trials of life work patience in my life. Likewise, patience leads to experience and experience leads to hope.[12] Thank you, Lord. Teach me not to grow weary in well-doing as I realize that I will reap in due season if I will learn to wait for your perfect will to be accomplished in my life.[13] Teach me to be patient toward all other people in my life, Lord.[14] Let the fruit of your Spirit fill me with patience.[15]

As your coming draws nigh, O Lord, I know that I need to learn how to be swift to hear, slow to speak, and slow to become angry.[16] Give me strong patience, Father, so that I will be able to endure and persevere in all situations.[17] I know that it is acceptable to you, Father, if when I do well and still suffer for it, taking it patiently all the while, that I stand fast in hope and trust.[18] One day with you is as a thousand years and a thousand years are as one day to you, Lord.[19] Help me to be more like you.

References: *(1) Galatians 5:22; (2) Hebrews 10:36; (3) Psalms 130:5; (4) Psalms 18:30; (5) Psalms 33:20; (6) Psalms 130:6; (7) Proverbs 14:29; (8) Ecclesiastes 7:8; (9) Isaiah 25:9; (10) Habakkuk 2:3; (11) Psalms 119:90; (12) Romans 5:3-4; (13) Galatians 6:9; (14) 1 Thessalonians 5:14; (15) Galatians 5:22; (16) James 1:19; (17) James 5:11; (18) 1 Peter 2:20; (19) 2 Peter 3:8.*

The Power of Agreement

Key Thought: The power of agreement is the power of unity.

Key Scripture: *"Assuredly, I say to you, Whatever you bind on earth will be bound in heaven, and whatever you loose on earth will be loosed in heaven. Again I say to you that if two of you agree on earth concerning anything that they ask, it will be done for them by my Father in heaven. For where two or three are gathered together in My name, I am there in the midst of them" (Matt. 18:19-20, NKJV).*

Prayer: Lord, teach me to agree with you in all things, for this is the confidence that I have in you, that if I will ask anything according to your will, I know you will hear me. Likewise, I know that because you hear my prayers, you will grant to me the petitions I have desired.[1] Thank you for this wonderful confidence that enables me to come boldly before your throne in order to find grace and mercy to help me in my time of need.[2]

Lord, I desire to be in agreement with you and my fellow-believers at all times. Your Word declares that it is good and pleasant for brethren to dwell together in unity.[3] I pray for the unity that you value so highly to be actualized in my relationships with other believers and with you. I pray that I would be one with you and one with other

Christians so that the power of agreeing prayer could be realized in our present time.[4]

I agree with your Word, Father. I realize that it contains your whole counsel.[5] It shows me how I should pray,[6] how I should live,[7] and how I should believe.[8] Teach me your perfect way in all things, Lord.[9]

Thank you for your promise, heavenly Father, that if two of us shall agree as touching anything we ask, it shall be done by you.[10] Lead me to a prayer partner, Lord, who will pray the prayer of agreement with me regularly. Your Word assures me that one believer is able to chase a thousand enemies, and two in agreement can put ten thousand to flight.[11] All the prayer promises of your Word are so precious to me; I thank you that you will never permit your Word to return unto you void, but it will accomplish whatever you desire, and it will prosper in the thing for which you sent it.[12]

Lord, when I work together with you — in prayer, in witnessing, in service, and in warfare — so many wonderful things are accomplished. I thank you that I am a joint-heir with Jesus and a co-laborer with you.[13] Thank you for the power of agreement in my life.

References: (1) 1 John 5:14-15; (2) Hebrews 4:16; (3) Psalms 133:1; (4) John 17:21; (5) Acts 20:27; (6) Luke 11:1-4; (7) Romans 6:8; (8) Romans 10:17; (9) Psalms 86:11; (10) Matthew 18:19-20; (11) Deuteronomy 32:30; (12) Isaiah 55:11; (13) Romans 8:17.

Power to Witness

Key Thought: Every person needs to know Jesus, or to know Him better.

Key Scripture: *"But you shall receive power when the Holy Spirit has come upon you; and you shall be witnesses to Me in Jerusalem, and in all Judea and Samaria, and to the end of the earth" (Acts 1:8, NKJV).*

Prayer: Heavenly Father, thank you for sending your Son, my Lord and Savior Jesus Christ, to be the sacrifice for my sins and the sins of others.[1] How I thank you that He is our Advocate,[2] the Mediator between us and you,[3] and how I thank you that He ever lives to make intercession for the saints according to your will.[4] Jesus is the same today, yesterday, and forever;[5] He will never leave me nor forsake me.[6] Thank you, Father, for giving your only begotten Son so that whoever would believe in Him would not perish, but have eternal life.[7]

Help me to be a faithful witness for you, Lord, it is my heart-felt desire to help to fulfill your Great Commission to go into all the world and preach your gospel,[8] for the Gospel of Jesus Christ is your power unto salvation to all who believe.[9] I ask you to enable me to speak you Word with great boldness,[10] and to proclaim the Word of life; I know that by doing so I will rejoice in the day of Christ, certain that I have not run in vain nor labored in vain.[11] Thank you for the certainty that comes through faith in your Word.

Let me boldly proclaim that it is by grace through faith that we are saved, and that this is not of ourselves, it is your gift to us.[12] Thank you, Father. I want to be your ambassador, always looking for those who will receive Jesus as their Savior, because as many as receive Him will also have your power to become your children because they believe on the name of Jesus. Such people are born of you, Father.[13] Lead me to those who need to know you, to those who need to realize that they must be born again in order to see your Kingdom.[14] I praise you, Lord, that the Word was made flesh and dwelt among us. I have beheld His glory, the glory as of your only begotten Son, full of grace and truth.[15] Of His fullness I have received, and grace for grace.[16] Praise you, Lord.

Help me always to remember that the wages of sin are death, but your gift is eternal life to all who believe in your Son.[17] Thank you so much for commending your love toward us, in that while we were yet sinners, your Son, Jesus Christ my Lord, died for us.[18] Let me love others with His love because He first loved me.[19]

References: *(1) 1 John 2:2; (2) 1 John 2:1; (3) 1 Timothy 2:5; (4) Romans 8:27; (5) Hebrews 13:8; (6) Hebrews 13:5; (7) John 3:16; (8) Matthew 28:19-20; (9) Romans 1:16; (10) Acts 4:29; (11) Philippians 2:16; (12) Ephesians 2:8-9; (13) John 1:12; (14) John 3:3; (15) John 1:14; (16) John 1:16; (17) Romans 6:23; (18) Romans 5:8; (19) 1 John 4:19.*

Practicing God's Presence

Key Thought: He is the God who is always there.

Key Scripture: *"Now therefore, I pray, if I have found grace in Your sight, show me now Your way, that I may know You and that I may find grace in Your sight....And He said, 'My Presence will go with you, and I will give you rest'" (Exod. 33:13-14, NKJV).*

Prayer: Lord God, you are a very present help to me.[1] You will never leave me nor forsake me.[2] You are the same yesterday, today, and forever,[3] and you will be with me until the end of the age.[4] I thank you for your abiding presence in my life. It is my heart's greatest desire to abide in you and to let your words abide in me. Thank you that such abiding brings wonderful answers to my prayers.[5] Thank you for your faithfulness; truly, Father, your lovingkindness is better than life to me.[6]

Glory and honor are in your presence; strength and gladness come from you.[7] You are showing me the path of life; in your presence there is fullness of joy; at your right hand there are pleasures forevermore.[8] I want to learn to live fully in your presence each day, Lord.

I will ever sing to you, and make a joyful noise to you, because you are the rock of my salvation. I come before your presence with thanksgiving and make a joyful noise to you with psalms because you are a great God, the King of kings.[9] I serve you with gladness, Lord, and I enter your presence with singing because I know you are my God. You have made me; I am a sheep in your pasture. Therefore, I enter your gates with thanksgiving, and I go into your courts with praise. I am thankful to you and I bless your name. You are so good to me, Lord; your mercy is everlasting, and your truth endures to all generations.[10]

Create in me a clean heart, O God; and renew a right spirit within me. Never cast me away from your presence, and do not take your Holy Spirit from me. It is my desire to teach transgressors your ways so that sinners will be converted unto you.[11] How sweet are the times of refreshing that come when I am restfully abiding in your wonderful presence, O Lord.[12]

When I am in your presence, Father, I realize how wonderful it is that I have life in Christ Jesus who is my wisdom, righteousness, sanctification, and redemption. Such knowledge helps me to know that I have no glory in myself, but I am able to glory in you.[13]

References: *(1) Psalms 46:1; (2) Hebrews 13:5; (3) Hebrews 13:8; (4) Matthew 28:20; (5) John 15:7; (6) Psalms 63:3; (7) 1 Chronicles 16:27; (8) Psalms 16:11; (9) Psalms 95:1-3; (10) Psalms 100; (11) Psalms 51:10-13; (12) Acts 3:19; (13) 1 Corinthians 1:29-31.*

Promise-Keeping

Key Thought: The first step in trust-building is promise-keeping.

Key Scripture: *"When you make a vow to the Lord your God, you shall not delay to pay it; for the Lord your God will surely require it of you, and it would be sin to you. But if you abstain from vowing, it shall not be sin to you"* *(Deut. 23:21-22, NKJV).*

Prayer: Heavenly Father, I thank you for your great faithfulness to me.[1] You never fail to keep your promises.[2] Your Word is true,[3] and you will never break your covenant with your people.[4] What you say, you will do, and you will make good everything you speak.[5] All of your promises come to pass in our lives, and not one of them has ever failed.[6] Help me to be like you; I never want to go back on my word to you or to anyone.[7] Help me walk in the Spirit, Lord, so that I will be ever faithful.[8]

I commit myself to keeping my vows to you, Lord. I will not defer to keep my vows.[9] You are never slack concerning your promise, and I don't ever want to be slack either.[10] How I praise you for your covenant to me; you will not forsake me nor destroy me, and you will never forget your covenant with those you love.[11] Like you, Lord, I want always to be a promise-keeper.

Heavenly Father, I resolve to be faithful in keeping all of my promises to my spouse,[12] my children,[13] my employer,[14] my church and pastor,[15] my friends, and others.[16] Most importantly, I promise to love you with all my heart, soul, mind, and strength, and to love my neighbor as myself.[17] I determine also to obey your Great Commision to preach the gospel and make disciples.[18]

Not one word of your promises has ever failed.[19] You will always be mindful of your covenant.[20] You have promised to always be my God and I will always be your child.[21] Help me always to remember, Lord, that a covenant involves two parties keeping their promises to each other. I always want to do my part by honoring you,[22] obeying you,[23] and telling others about you.[24]

I join myself to you, Lord.[25] Thank you for the new covenant through the blood of Jesus Christ, and for all you have done for me.[26] Hallelujah!

References: *(1) Lamentations 3:23; (2) Numbers 23:19; (3) Psalms 18:30; (4) Ezekiel 24:14; (5) Numbers 23:19; (6) Joshua 23:14; (7) Judges 11:35; (8) Galatians 5:16; (9) Ecclesiastes 5:4; (10) 2 Peter 3:9; (11) Deuteronomy 4:31; (12) Ephesians 5:31; (13) Psalms 127:3; (14) Ephesians 6:5; (15) 1 Corinthians 12:13; (16) Galatians 6:2; (17) Mark 12:30-31; (18) Matthew 28:19-20; (19) 1 King 8:56; (20) Psalms 111:5; (21); Jeremiah 30:22; (22) Proverbs 3:9; (23) Psalms 18:44; (24) Matthew 28:19-20; (25) Jeremiah 50:5; (26) 1 Corinthians 11:25.*

Putting on the Armor of God

Key Thought: Nothing can penetrate God's protective armor.

Key Scripture: *"Put on the whole armor of God, that you may be able to stand against the wiles of the devil" (Eph. 6:11, NKJV).*

Prayer: Thank you for providing me with your protective armor, Father, as I go forth in spiritual warfare daily. I want to wear each piece of armor every moment; help me to remember to put on each piece every morning carefully, with prayer. I will pray always with all prayer and supplication in the Spirit, and I will watch thereunto with all perseverance and supplication for all saints.[1] Even as I pray for others, Father, I pray also for myself, that your utterance would be given to me so that I would be able to open my mouth boldly, making known the mystery of your gospel to all those with whom I come in contact.[2]

Thank you for making me your ambassador. Teach me to speak boldly as I know I ought to speak.[3] I will be strong in you and in the power of your might as I wear the protective armor you have supplied to me.[4] With your armor on, I will be able to stand against the wiles of the devil,[5] for you are with me and you will never leave me nor forsake me.[6]

Help me always to be cognizant of the fact that I do not wrestle against flesh and blood, but against principalities, powers, rulers of this world's darkness, and spiritual wickedness in high places.[7]

As I go forth in battle against these forces, constantly remind me that the weapons of my warfare are not carnal, but they are mighty through you to the pulling down of strongholds. Guide me, Lord, in this aggressive and militant work of casting down imaginations, and everything that exalts itself against the all-important knowledge of you. Help me to work with you by bringing into captivity every thought to the obedience of Christ.[8]

Wherefore I now take unto myself the whole armor you have provided for me so that I will be able to stand in the evil day.[9] I gird my loins with your truth and I put on the breastplate of your righteousness.[10] I put on the shoes of the preparation of your gospel of peace.[11] Above all, I take the shield of faith with which I will quench all the fiery darts of the wicked one.[12] I take the helmet of salvation to protect my mind,[13] and the sword of your Spirit, which is your Word.[14] Now, Lord, I am ready to stand upon your promises, realizing that nothing that happens today will be able to penetrate your perfect armor.

References: *(1) Ephesians 6:18; (2) Ephesians 6:19; (3) Ephesians 6:20; (4) Ephesians 6:10; (5) Ephesians 6:11; (6) Hebrews 13:5; (7) Ephesians 6:12; (8) 2 Corinthians 10:5; (9) Ephesians 6:13; (10) Ephesians 6:14; (11) Ephesians 6:15; (12) Ephesians 6:16; (13) Ephesians 6:17; (14) Ephesians 6:17.*

Repentance

Key Thought: "True repentance is to cease from sin" (St. Ambrose).

Key Scripture: *"The Lord your God is gracious and merciful, and will not turn His face from you if you return to Him" (2 Chron. 30:9, NKJV).*

Prayer: Thank you, heavenly Father, for the gift of repentance,[1] for leading me to be sorry for my sins and to want to change my behavior in ways that will please you. Forgive, I pray, my sins of _____ _____. I truly repent, and I determine to walk away from my sins with your help.[2]

The blood of your Son, my Lord and Savior Jesus Christ, makes atonement for my soul.[3] I confess my sins to you in the full realization that you are faithful and just to forgive all my sins and to cleanse me from all unrighteousness.[4] Thank you, Father. I truly desire to turn from all evil ways and to keep your commandments and statutes at all times.[5] As your Word points out, to depart from evil is understanding,[6] and I want that kind of wisdom, Father.

Thank you for the continuing assurance that if I will turn to you, Lord, you will have mercy upon me.[7] I recognize my need for your mercy, grace, and forgiveness,[8] and

I thank you for your love.[9] By seeking you I find real and abundant life.[10]

Help me, Lord God, to bring forth fruits that are worthy of repentance.[11] I ask that even the thoughts of my heart would be forgiven[12] as I endeavor to live a righteous, pure, and holy life through your power.[13]

How I praise you, Father, for your goodness that leads me to repentance.[14] Your goodness imparts so many wonderful blessings to my life.

I pray that you would endue your ministers with power from on high so that they would be enabled to preach repentance and remission of sins in your name among all nations.[15] Your Son has not come to call the righteous, but sinners to repentance.[16] Convict people of their sins and convince them of their need for your righteousness so that they will truly repent. I thank you for the joy that exists in heaven over every sinner that repents.[17] Certainly I am experiencing that joy even now as I realize how wonderful it is that you have forgiven me and restored me to fellowship with you. Thank you, Lord.

References: *(1) Acts 5:31; (2) Ezekiel 18:30; (3) Leviticus 17:11; (4) 1 John 1:9; (5) 2 Kings 17:13; (6) Job 28:28; (7) Isaiah 55:7; (8) Psalms 94:18; (9) 1 John 4:8; (10) Amos 5:6; (11) Luke 3:8; (12) Acts 8:22; (13) Colossians 1:11; (14) Romans 2:4; (15) Luke 24:47; (16) Matthew 9:13; (17) Luke 15:7.*

Restoration of the Weary Soul

Key Thought: God wants you to experience wholeness.

Key Scripture: *"Be glad then, you children of Zion, And rejoice in the Lord your God: For He has given you the former rain faithfully, And He will cause the rain to come down for you — The former rain, And the latter rain in the first month. The threshing floors shall be full of wheat, And the vats shall overflow with new wine and oil. So I will restore to you the years that the swarming locust has eaten, the crawling locust, the consuming locust, and the chewing locust, My great army which I sent among you. You shall eat in plenty and be satisfied, And praise the name of the Lord your God" (Joel 2:23-26, NKJV).*

Prayer: Father, I have grown weary in the journey of life, and in the process I feel that I've lost so much. I come to you now, asking you to restore to me the joy of your salvation,[1] and to help me to recover from the mistakes and losses that have accumulated in my life.

Thank you for your promise that the desert shall rejoice and blossom like the rose once more.[2] You are my hope, O Lord God, and I place my trust in you.[3] Open my eyes, Lord, so that I will be able to behold wondrous things from your Word.[4] Open my ears so that I will be able to discern your voice when you speak to me.[5] Thank you, Father, for hearing my prayer and for bringing restoration to my soul.[6]

I wait upon you, O Lord, because I know that as I wait, you will renew my strength.[7] I thank you for your promise that the old things are passed away, and you make all things new.[8] Renew me in the spirit of my mind,[9] and help me to put on the new man.[10]

Forgive me, Father, for my sins of omission and commission. I specifically repent now of the following:

_____

_____. Thank you for granting repentance to my heart,[11] and for forgiving me of my sins and cleansing me from all unrighteousness.[12]

Thank you for your promise to restore health to me and to heal me of all my wounds.[13] How I thank you for your promise that you will restore all things.[14] I believe the promises of your Word, and I determine to obey you in all things. You give me beauty for ashes, the oil of joy for mourning, the garment of praise for the spirit of heaviness, so that I may be called a tree of righteousness, the planting of the Lord, that you may be glorified, O Lord.[15] I will greatly rejoice in you, Lord; my soul will be joyful in you, my God, for you have clothed me with the garments of salvation and with the robe of righteousness.[16] Lord, I draw close to you now and I receive the refreshing that comes from being in your presence.[17] Thank you for your blessing of rest, renewal, recovery, refreshing, and total restoration.

References: *(1) Psalms 51:12; (2) Isaiah 35:1; (3) Psalms 71:5; (4) Psalms 119:18; (5) John 10:27; (6) Psalms 23:3; (7) Isaiah 40:31; (8) 2 Corinthians 5:17; (9) Ephesians 4:23; (10) Ephesians 4:24; (11) Acts 5:31; (12) 1 John 1:9; (13) Jeremiah 30:17; (14) Mark 9:12; (15) Isaiah 61:3; (16) Isaiah 61:10; (17) Acts 3:19.*

Returning to the Father

Key Thought: Our God is a loving heavenly Father.

Key Scripture: *"As a father pities his children, So the Lord pities those who fear Him. for He knows our frame; He remembers that we are dust" (Ps. 103:13-14, NKJV).*

Prayer: Father, I thank you for your promises. I believe that anyone who comes to you will in no wise be cast out.[1] I recognize that Jesus is the way, the truth, and the life, and no one can come to you except by Him.[2] I, therefore, come to you now, through Jesus Christ, asking you to forgive my sins and to cleanse me from all unrighteousness.[3] I want to return to your perfect way.[4]

Like a sheep, I have gone astray, Lord.[5] Having begun true life in the Spirit, somehow I became sidetracked and began to believe that I could become righteous through the flesh.[6] Forgive me, Father. I thank you for your goodness that leads me to repentance.[7] Truly, I do repent, and I determine to walk after your Spirit instead of after the flesh.[8] I now remember from whence I have fallen, and I repent, Lord.[9] Thank you for granting repentance to my heart.[10]

I come to you, Father, realizing that I have sinned against heaven and before you. In spite of this, Lord, I know that you do have compassion on me. Thank you for your kiss of love. Like the Prodigal Son, I have sinned, but I know you rejoice as I return to you.[11] Thank you, Lord, for your love. I love you because you first loved me.[12]

In returning and in rest I know I shall be saved.[13] Thank you, Lord, for making provision for me. Unto your salvation I was called, Lord. Thank you for the example of my Lord and Savior, Jesus Christ, who suffered for me, and left me an example, that I should follow in His steps. He did no sin, neither was there any guile found in His mouth. When He was reviled, He did not revile in return. When He suffered, He did not threaten. Instead, He committed himself to you, Father, because He knew you judge right-eously. Thank you for His willingness to bear my sins in His own body on the tree, so that I, being dead to my sins, could live unto righteousness. By His stripes I am healed. I was like a sheep that had gone astray, but now I am returning to the Shepherd and Bishop of my soul.[14] Thank you, Father, for accepting me into your beloved.[15]

References: *(1) John 6:37; (2) John 14:6; (3) 1 John 1:9; (4) Psalms 18:30; (5) Isaiah 53:6; (6) Galatians 3:3; (7) Romans 2:4; (8) Romans 8:1; (9) Revelation 2:5; (10) Acts 5:31; (11) Luke 15:18-32; (12) 1 John 4:19; (13) Isaiah 30:15; (14) 1 Peter 2:25; (15) Ephesians 1:6.*

A Searching Heart

Key Thought: A seeking heart always finds the truth.

Key Scripture: *"When You said, 'Seek My face,' My heart said to You, 'Your face, Lord, I will seek.' Do not hide Your face from me; Do not turn Your servant away in anger; You have been my help; Do not leave me nor forsake me, O God of my salvation" (Ps. 27:8-9, NKJV).*

Prayer: As the deer pants for the water brooks, so does my heart pant after you, O Lord.[1] Your promise declares that I will always find you if I seek you with all my heart and all my soul.[2] I choose always to search for you in every situation, Father, to look for your truth, and as I do so, I know I will find you.[3] You will lead me and guide me into all truth,[4] as I search the Scriptures daily in the way you have commanded me to do.[5]

When you said to me, "Seek my face," my heart responded, "Your face, O Lord, I will seek."[6] When I look unto you, I become radiant because the light of your countenance shines upon me.[7] Lift up the light of your countenance upon me, and give me your peace.[8] You are my glory and the lifter of my head.[9] As I look up, I realize that my help comes from you.[10] You are the Maker of heaven and earth, and as I look up, I realize that my redemption draws nigh.[11]

In the broad ways of life, I will always seek you, Lord, because you are the One my soul truly loves.[12] I will seek you while you may be found; I will call upon you while you are near.[13] I will search for you with all my heart,[14] because in times like these it is so very important to seek you.[15] I will seek good, and not evil, so that I will be able to live fully.[16] Thank you for the abundant life you have promised to me.[17]

I thank you for your Spirit who searches all things.[18] I ask Him to search my heart, and to place His finger on any area of my life that I need to change,[19] so that I will be able to seek you more fully. I thank you that you are the One who searches the minds and the hearts of your people.[20] Lord, I will seek first your kingdom, and your righteousness, and I know that you will provide me with all I need.[21]

References: *(1) Psalms 42:1; (2) Matthew 7:7; (3) 1 Chronicles 28:9; (4) John 16:13; (5) Acts 17:11; (6) Psalms 27:8; (7) Psalms 34:5; (8) Numbers 6:26; (9) Psalms 3:3; (10) Psalms 121:1-2; (11) John 4:35; (12) Song of Solomon 3:2; (13) Isaiah 55:6; (14) Jeremiah 29:13; (15) Hosea 10:12; (16) Amos 5:14; (17) John 10:10; (18) 1 Corinthians 2:10; (19) Psalms 139:23; (20) Revelation 2:23; (21) Matthew 6:33.*

A Servant's Heart

Key Thought: "The world cannot always understand one's profession of faith, but it can understand service" (Ian Maclaren).

Key Scripture: *"Well done, good and faithful servant; you were faithful over a few things, I will make you ruler over many things" (Matt. 25:21, NKJV).*

Prayer: Heavenly Father, I thank you for the opportunities I have to serve you in every area of my life — in my family, my church, my community, and my work. Speak, Lord, for your servant wants to hear you.[1] Direct me into pathways of service so that I would be able to please you.

Father, I want to serve you with all my heart and soul.[2] Help me to serve you with a perfect heart and a willing mind.[3] Teach me to minister to you,[4] to serve you with gladness, and to come before your presence with singing.[5] I want to serve my Lord and Savior, Jesus Christ, with all my heart and I thank you, Father, for your promise to honor me as I do so.[6] Help me always to serve in newness of spirit, not in the oldness of the letter.[7]

Here I am; send me, Father.[8] I desire to be used by you in service to mankind as I serve you in sincerity and truth.[9] A servant who comes in your name, Lord, is blessed and happy.[10] Thank you for the happiness that comes to me when I am in your service. The fields are white unto harvest, Lord, and I want to be your servant in this time of harvest.[11]

I have received from you so freely, and because of your blessings in my life, I want to serve you freely by giving to others what you have given to me.[12] Anoint me, I pray, to feed your lambs and your sheep.[13] So fill me with your Spirit, Lord, that I would be able to serve you with all humility of mind, even if it requires many tears.[14] I want to labor together in tandem with you, Father.[15] Lead me to be all things to all people so that I might, by all means, be able to save some.[16]

Build stability in my life, Lord, so that I will always be steadfast, unmovable, truly abounding in your work, for I know that my labors will never be in vain when I am in you.[17] I desire to be an ambassador for Christ,[18] to do good to all people,[19] to be a peacemaker,[20] to feed your flock,[21] and to be forgiving and tender-hearted to your people.[22]

I delight myself in you, Lord, knowing that you will give me the desires of my heart. I commit my way to you and I trust you to bring these things to pass.[23]

References: *(1) 1 Samuel 3:9; (2) Deuteronomy 10:12; (3) 1 Chronicles 28:9; (4) 2 Chronicles 29:11; (5) Psalms 100:2; (6) John 12:26; (7) Romans 7:6; (8) Isaiah 6:8; (9) Joshua 24:14; (10) Psalms 118:26; (11) Matthew 9:37; (12) Matthew 10:8; (13) John 21:15-17; (14) Acts 20:19; (15) 1 Corinthians 3:9; (16) 1 Corinthians 9:22; (17) 1 Corinthians 15:58; (18) 2 Corinthians 5:20; (19) Galatians 6:10; (20) Matthew 5:9; (21) 1 Peter 5:2; (22) Ephesians 4:32; (23) Psalms 37:4-5.*

A Spiritual Perspective

Key Thought: "The spirit of man is the candle of the Lord" (Prov. 20:27).

Key Scripture: *"For they that are after the flesh do mind the things of the flesh; but they that are after the Spirit the things of the Spirit. For to be carnally minded is death; but to be spiritually minded is life and peace" (Rom. 8:5-6).*

Prayer: My Father in heaven, I praise you for all the spiritual resources you have provided for me to live effectively in this present world.[1] Because the Spirit of Christ dwells in me, my mortal body is quickened,[2] my mind is renewed,[3] and I am seated in the heavenly places where I can see things from your point of view.[4]

Because of your mercies to me, I present my life to you as a living sacrifice, holy, and acceptable unto you. This is simply reasonable service — the least that I can do — when I consider all your mercies and all that you have done for me.[5] Help me, Lord, not to be conformed to this world, but rather to be transformed by the renewing of my mind. It is my desire, Father, to prove what is your good and acceptable and perfect will.[6]

Close up the gap between my ways and your ways, and between my thoughts and your thoughts[7] as I draw closer to you.   Thank you for always responding by drawing closer to me, Father.[8]

Let the mind of Christ be formed in me. How I thank you that even though He was in your form, O Lord, He thought it not robbery to be equal with you, but at the same time made himself of no reputation, and took upon himself the form of a servant, and was made in the likeness of sinful men. He humbled himself and became obedient unto death, even the death of the cross.[9]

I want to value the same things you value, Lord. I seek first your kingdom and your righteousness, and in doing so, I know that all these other things will be added unto me.[10] Thank you for all the wonderful promises of your Word, Father.

Fill me with the knowledge of your will in all wisdom and spiritual understanding so that I might walk worthy of you unto all pleasing, being fruitful in every good work, and increasing in your knowledge. Strengthen me with all might, according to your glorious power, unto all patience with joyfulness. I give thanks unto you, Father, for you have made it possible for me to become a partaker of the inheritance of the saints in light and you have delivered me from the power of darkness.[11] Thank you for my redemption that was purchased by the precious blood of my Lord and Savior, Jesus Christ.[12]

References: *(1) Titus 2:12; (2) Romans 8:11; (3) Romans 12:2; (4) Ephesians 2:6; (5) Romans 12:1; (6) Romans 12:2; (7) Isaiah 55:8-9; (8) James 4:8; (9) Philippians 2:5-8; (10) Matthew 6:33; (11) Colossians 1:9-13; (12) Colossians 1:14.*

Standing on the Promises

Key Thought: Focus on the promises of God, not on the problems of life.

Key Scripture: *"Behold, this day I am going the way of all the earth. And you know in all your hearts and in all your souls that not one thing has failed of all the good things which the Lord your God spoke concerning you. All have come to pass for you; not one word of them has failed" (Josh. 23:14, NKJV).*

Prayer: Lord God, Maker of heaven and earth, I come to you now to thank you for your great and precious promises,[1] and to covenant with you to take my stand and to stake my life on your promises to me. Your Word will never return to you void;[2] you are always faithful to fulfill your promises to your people;[3] therefore, I know that the blessings you have promised will come to pass. Thank you for all the good things you have brought to me; your promises will never fail.[4]

Your hand, dear Father, has never been shortened.[5] You always do what you promise, and when you speak, you always make it good.[6] Help me to be faithful like you, Lord, so that I will never fail to pay a vow that I make in your presence.[7] You are never slack concerning your promises, Lord,[8] and I thank you so much for all the precious prayer promises I find in your Word.[9] You have promised me that if I will ask anything in your name, you will accomplish it.[10] I believe your promise, Lord.

I am filled with awe and wonder when I realize that you truly are able to do exceeding abundantly above all that I can ask or think.[11] You have called me, Father, and you are faithful to complete the work you have begun in my life.[12] Because you are faithful, I will not worry about anything, but in everything by prayer and supplication with thanksgiving in my heart, I will let my requests be made known unto you. In so doing, your wonderful peace that passes all understanding will keep my heart and mind through Christ Jesus.[13] I know that He will make it possible for me to receive wonderful answers from you, Lord; whatever I ask in His name shall be accomplished.[14]

All of your promises in Christ Jesus are yes and amen, unto your glory.[15] You, God, are my rock; in you I will trust. You are my shield and the horn of my salvation, my high tower, my refuge, my Savior, and you save me from violence. I will ever call upon you, Lord, because you are worthy to be praised, and I know that by so doing I will be saved from my enemies.[16]

References: *(1) 2 Peter 1:4; (2) Isaiah 55:11; (3) 1 Thessalonians 5:24; (4) Joshua 23:14;(5) Numbers 11:23; (6) Numbers 23:19; (7) Deuteronomy 23:21; (8) 2 Peter 3:9; (9) 2 Peter 1:4; (10) John 14:14; (11) Ephesians 3:20-21; (12) 1 Thessalonians 5:24; (13) Philippians 4:6-7; (14) John 16:23; (15) 2 Corinthians 1:20; (16) 2 Samuel 22:3-4.*

Strength

Key Thought: God perfects His strength during our times of weakness.

Key Scripture: *"The Lord is my strength and song, and he is become my salvation: he is my God, and I will prepare him an habitation; my father's God, and I will exalt him. The Lord is a man of war: the Lord is his name"* *(Exod. 15:2-3).*

Prayer: Lord God of strength and power, I thank you for your omnipotence (all-powerfulness). Your strength is made perfect in my times of weakness.[1] Your joy is my strength.[2] Your right hand has become glorious in power, and it has dashed the enemy into pieces.[3] You are my strength, and you are my shield.[4] Blessed be your name, O Lord; you teach my hands to war and my fingers to fight.[5]

Help me ever to remember that the race is not to the swift, nor the battle to the strong, but you, Lord-Jehovah, are the source of all my strength.[6] I will trust in you forever because I know that in you there is everlasting strength.[7] Help me to rest in such certainty, Lord, fully realizing that it is in quietness and in confidence that I will obtain strength.[8]

Thank you for fighting for me.[9] Ultimately, I realize that the battle is not mine; it is yours, so I ask that you will help me to set myself to stand fast and to see your salvation in the midst of every battle.[10] You are sweeter than honey and you are stronger than a lion.[11] Your ways are strength to me,[12] and your Word keeps me from sin.[13] I praise you, Father, for your strength and your love.

I recognize the value of wisdom that you impart to me through your Word, Father. It is a source of strength to me.[14] Indeed, wisdom is even better than strength.[15] Wisdom and might are yours, Lord,[16] and the people who know you shall be strong and they will do mighty exploits in your name.[17] I want to be such a person, Father; thank you for leading me to know you and to find your strength to empower my life.

You, Lord God, are my strength.[18] By your Spirit I shall prevail.[19] Your "weakness" is stronger than men,[20] and your strength is made perfect in man's weakness. Because this is true, I know that when I am weak I shall be strong because you are with me,[21] and I will be strong in you, Lord, and in the power of your might.[22]

References: (1) 2 Corinthians 12:9; (2) Nehemiah 8:10; (3) Exodus 15:6; (4) Psalms 28:7; (5) Psalms 144:1; (6) Ecclesiastes 9:11; (7) Isaiah 26:4; (8) Isaiah 30:15; (9) Joshua 23:10; (10) 1 Samuel 17:47; (11) Judges 14:18; (12) Proverbs 10:29; (13) Psalms 119:11; (14) Ecclesiastes 7:19; (15) Ecclesiastes 9:16; (16) Daniel 2:20; (17) Daniel 11:32; (18) Habakkuk 3:19; (19) Zechariah 4:6; (20) 1 Corinthians 1:25; (21) 2 Corinthians 12:10; (22) Ephesians 6:10.*

Strength of Character

Key Thought: "Character is destiny" (George Eliot).

Key Scripture: *"And he said to me, 'My grace is sufficient for you, for My strength is made perfect in weakness.' Therefore most gladly I will rather boast in my infirmities, that the power of Christ may rest upon me. Therefore I take pleasure in infirmities, in reproaches, in needs, in persecutions, in distresses, for Christ's sake. For when I am weak, then I am strong"* (2 Cor. 12:9-10, NKJV).

Prayer: Lord, I thank you and praise you for the strength of character you are forming in my life by your grace. Lord, you are my strength and my shield.[1] You are my strength and my song and you have become my salvation.[2] Because this is true, I know that you are building strong character and discipline within me to enable me to face my weaknesses and struggles in the following areas of my life:_____.
I renounce these weaknesses in your name, Lord. I repent of my sins in these areas, and I covenant before you that I will walk away from them by trusting in your strength. Following your way is strength to me.[3]

Your divine power gives me all the things that pertain to life and godliness as a result of knowing you. Thank you for calling me to glory and the virtue of strong character.[4] I want the virtue of strong character to be in evidence in my life.

I will trust in you forever, because in you, O Lord, there is everlasting strength.[5] Wisdom and might are yours, and I want to learn how to lean on you when areas of weakness are exposed in my life.[6] Help me to walk in the Spirit and not fulfill the lusts of the flesh.[7]

Thank you for giving power to me when I feel weak and for increasing your strength in me when I feel I have no strength to face temptation or to endure hardship in my life.[8] Lord, I want to learn how to trust in you at all times instead of leaning on my own understanding. In all my ways I want to acknowledge you, and in so doing, I know you will direct my paths.[9]

I resolve before you, Lord, to walk in the integrity of my heart.[10] I want other people to know that I am person who keeps the commitments and promises I make, a faithful person who keeps my word at all times.[11] Let the integrity you have imparted to my heart guide me at all times.[12]

When I come to the end of my course, I want to be able to say, "I have lived in all good conscience before God until this day."[13]

What you, Lord, say to me, that will I speak.[14] Give me the light to always walk as a child of your light, Father.[15] The righteousness you have given to me I will never forsake, and my heart shall not reproach me as long as I live, because, you, O Lord, have given strength of character to me.[16]

References: *(1) Psalms 28:7; (2) Exodus 15:2; (3) Proverbs 10:29; (4) 2 Peter 1:3; (5) Isaiah 26:4; (6) Daniel 2:20; (7) Galatians 5:16; (8) Isaiah 40:29; (9) Proverbs 3:5-6; (10) Psalms 26:11; (11) Proverbs 14:5; (12) Proverbs 11:3; (13) Acts 23:1; (14) 1 Kings 22:14; (15) Ephesians 5:8; (16) Job 27:6.*

Teach Me Your Way

Key Thought: "The greatest good is wisdom" (St. Augustine).

Key Scripture: *"Teach me Your way, O Lord, And lead me in a smooth path, because of my enemies,...Wait on the Lord; Be of good courage, And He shall strengthen your heart; Wait, I say, on the Lord.'" (Ps. 27:11-14, NKJV).*

Prayer: Lord, your way is perfect. Your Word is tried. You are a buckler to all those who trust in you.[1] You are my Rock and my fortress. You are my Deliverer, my strength, and the horn of my salvation. I call upon you because I know you are worthy to be praised, and in so doing, I know I shall be saved from my enemies.[2]

Lord, you are good and upright. Because of your goodness, you are teaching me your ways.[3] Unto you, therefore, I lift up my soul. O my God, I trust in you. Show me your ways, O Lord, and teach me your paths.[4] Lead me in your truth and teach me, for you are the God of my salvation. I wait on you all day.[5]

Help me to walk in meekness so that I will be able to learn your ways.[6] You are my hiding place, and I know you will preserve me from trouble. Compass me about with songs of deliverance, and instruct me and teach me in your way. Thank you for guiding me with your eye, O Lord.[7]

Your eye is always upon one who reveres you; Lord, I revere, adore, and honor you, and I ever hope in your mercy. I know you will deliver my soul from death and keep me alive in times of want. My soul waits for you, because you are my help and my shield.[8]

In the day of trouble I will call upon you because I know you will answer me.[9] You are so very great, and you do wondrous things for me. You alone are God, so I ask you to teach me your ways. I will walk in the truth you reveal to me. Give me an undivided heart that I may revere your name at all times. I will praise you, O Lord my God, with all my heart, and I will glorify your name forevermore.[10] Great is your mercy to me, and you have delivered my soul from the lowest hell.[11]

Your way is strength to me.[12] Your fruit is better than gold, and your revenue is better than choice silver, Lord.[13] Lead me in the way of righteousness, in the midst of the paths of judgment so that I may be able to participate in all the blessings you promise to those who love you.[14]

References: *(1) Psalms 18:30; (2) Psalms 18:2-3; (3) Psalms 86:5; (4) Psalms 25:1-4; (5) Psalms 25:5; (6) Psalms 25:9; (7) Psalms 32:8; (8) Psalms 33:18-19; (9) Psalms 50:15; (10) Psalms 86:11-12; (11) Psalms 86:13; (12) Proverbs 10:29; (13) Proverbs 8:19; (14) Proverbs 8:20-21.*

Times of Adversity

Key Thought: Adversity reminds us of the things that really count in life.

Key Scripture: *"We are troubled on every side, yet not distressed; we are perplexed, but not in despair; Persecuted, but not forsaken; cast down, but not destroyed; Always bearing about in the body the dying of the Lord Jesus, that the life also of Jesus might be made manifest in our body" (2 Cor. 4:8-10).*

Prayer: Father, when tough times come, I am reminded of your promise that you will always be a very present help to me in times of trouble.[1] You will not leave me comfortless.[2] No temptation has overtaken me but such as is common to all; therefore, you will make a way for me to escape. Through your faithfulness to me, I will be able to endure.[3] Thank you, Lord.

Father, thank you for wanting to give me your kingdom.[4] I realize that it truly exists within me.[5] I'm thankful, Lord, that your kingdom does not consist of meat and drink, because it is righteousness, peace, and joy in your Holy Spirit.[6]

I realize I do not have anything to worry about, even in times of adversity, because you have invited me to cast all my care upon you.[7] How grateful I am, Lord, for your invitation to come to you when I feel overworked and stressed out. You have promised to give me your rest. I want to take your yoke upon me and to learn of you because I know that your burden is light.[8]

You are with me as I face the challenge of _____ _____ in my life right now. With complete confidence, therefore, I come before your throne, O Father, and I ask you to give me your mercy and grace to help me in this time of need.[9] Nothing is too hard for you, O Lord.[10] When I call upon you, you answer me and you show me great and mighty things which I could not otherwise know.[11] When I draw near to you, you always draw near to me.[12] Draw me, Lord, so that I can find that place of quiet rest near your heart.[13] Thank you for the peace that passes all understanding, even in the midst of difficult times.[14] Your love is stronger than death, and it is stronger than any circumstance of life.[15] Guide me in the way I should go.[16]

In my distress, I have cried to you, and I know you have heard me.[17] You are always near to all who call upon you in truth.[18] You always hear my cry,[19] and you never forget my need.[20] You have delivered me from all my fears,[21] turned my mourning into dancing,[22] and set me free from all oppression.[23] Thank you, Father; I will stand fast in the liberty that you have provided for me, and I will never again be entangled by the yoke of bondage that used to hold me back.[24]

References: *(1) Psalms 46:1; (2) John 14:18; (3) 1 Corinthians 10:13; (4) Luke 12:32; (5) Luke 17:21; (6) Romans 14:17; (7) 1 Peter 5:7; (8) Matthew 11:30; (9) Hebrews 4:16; (10) Genesis 18:14; (11) Jeremiah 33:3; (12) James 4:8; (13) Song of Solomon 1:4; (14) Philippians 4:7; (15) Romans 8:38-39; (16) Proverbs 3:5-6; (17) Psalms 120:1; (18) Psalms 145:18; (19) Job 34:28; (20) Psalms 9:12; (21) Psalms 34:4; (22) Psalms 30:11; (23) Galatians 5:1; (24) Galatians 5:1.*

Victory

Key Thought: You are a winner!

Key Scripture: *"These shall make war with the Lamb, and the Lamb shall overcome them: for he is Lord of lords, and King of kings: and they that are with him are called, and chosen, and faithful" (Rev. 17:14).*

Prayer: Heavenly Father, victory is yours. Through your Son, my Lord and Savior Jesus Christ, the battle is already won! How I thank you for the victory I have through Him.[1] Thank you for always being there to fight for me.[2] I will sing unto you, O Lord, for you have triumphed gloriously; the horse and the rider you have thrown into the sea.[3]

Your right hand, O Lord, has become glorious in power. Your right hand has dashed the enemy in pieces.[4] You have overthrown all who have risen against you, and you have sent forth your fiery wrath to consume them as stubble.[5] I praise you for your power, Father.

In the same way that David prevailed over the Philistine giant, you have given me the ability and strength to face the "giants" in my life.[6] I will not fear, for I know that you will deliver them into my hands.[7] You will save me from all my enemies and you will deliver me from all my problems.[8]

As you fought for Israel, I know you will fight for me.[9] I thank you, Lord, that the battle is not mine to fight by myself. By standing still and setting myself upon your foundation I will be able to stand fast and see your salvation come to pass.[10] Hallelujah! Such knowledge makes me feel like shouting.[11]

You are my Lord and you fight for me.[12] My enemies will never be able to triumph over me.[13] It is wonderful to know that I am able to overcome Satan by the blood of the Lamb that was slain for me from the foundation of the world.[14] Jesus has overcome the world,[15] and whatsoever is born of you overcomes the world as well.[16] Alleluia, for you, the Lord God omnipotent, reigns forever and ever.[17]

Through you, dear Father, a little one shall become a thousand, and a small one shall become as strong nation.[18] I implore you to make my enemies your footstool,[19] to let not the swift flee away or the mighty man escape your vengeance.[20] Thank you for your promise, Lord, that vengeance is yours; you will repay those who oppose you and your people.[21] This is the day that you have made, and I will rejoice and be glad in it,[22] for I know that no weapon that is formed against me will prosper, and every tongue that rises up against me in judgment will be condemned by you, for this is the heritage of the servants of the Lord, and their righteousness is from you.[23]

References: *(1) 1 Corinthians 15:57; (2) Exodus 14:14; (3) Exodus 15:1; (4) Exodus 15:6; (5) Exodus 15:7; (6) 1 Samuel 17:50; (7) Joshua 10:8; (8) Numbers 10:9; (9) Joshua 10:14; (10) 1 Samuel 2:1; (11) Joshua 6:16; (12) Joshua 23:10; (13) Psalms 41:11; (14) Revelation 12:11; (15) John 16:33; (16) 1 John 5:4; (17) Revelation 19:6; (18) Isaiah 60:22; (19) Psalms 110:1; (20) Jeremiah 46:6; (21) Romans 12:19; (22) Psalms 118:21; (23) Isaiah 54:17.*

Walking in Contentment

Key Thought: "A contented mind is the greatest blessing a man can enjoy in this world" (Joseph Addison).

Key Scripture: *"But godliness with contentment is great gain. For we brought nothing into this world, and it is certain we can carry nothing out. And having food and raiment let us be therewith content" (1 Tim. 6:6-8).*

Prayer: Teach me the true meaning of contentment, Lord. Teach me to be like the Apostle Paul who said, "Not that I speak in respect of want: for I have learned, in whatsoever state I am, therewith to be content."[1] Lord, I want to be like him. I want to know how to be abased and how to abound, to be full and to be hungry, to abound and to suffer need.[2] Contentment comes to me when I realize that I can endure and face anything through Christ Jesus who strengthens me.[3]

Even a meager portion, with the knowledge that you are with me, is better than great riches with trouble.[4] I recognize that godliness with contentment is great gain for me, Lord.[5] I thank you that you have permitted my eyes to behold your salvation, which you have prepared for your people, and this, Lord, brings contentment to my heart.[6] Through Jesus Christ, my Lord, I am able to have peace with you, Father.[7] Thank you for the blessings of contentment and peace. Truly, your peace passes all understanding.[8]

Let me be without covetousness at all times, Lord. Teach me to be content with such things as I have, realizing that the greatest blessing of all is that you will never leave me nor forsake me.[9] This truth brings great contentment to me, Lord. It enables me to know that you are my helper, and I do not have to fear what people can do to me.[10]

I find great contentment in your promise that your people will not hunger or thirst.[11] You never forsake the righteous, and the seed of the righteous will never have to beg for bread.[12] Lord, my cup overflows with the blessings you have given to me.[13] Thank you for giving me the more abundant life.[14] Truly, Lord, I know you to be the God of more than enough, the One who is ever able to do exceeding abundantly, beyond all that I can ask or think.[15] Thank you that you, Lord, live within me, and you are greater than he who is in the world.[16] You supply all of my needs according your riches in glory by Christ Jesus.[17]

References: (1) Philippians 4:11; (2) Philippians 4:12; (3) Philippians 4:13; (4) Proverbs 15:16; (5) 1 Timothy 6:6; (6) Luke 2:30-31; (7) Romans 5:1; (8) Philippians 4:7; (9) Hebrews 13:5; (10) Hebrews 13:6; (11) Revelation 7:16; (12) Psalms 37:25; (13) Psalms 23:5; (14) John 10:10; (15) Ephesians 3:20; (16) 1 John 4:4; (17) Philippians 4:19.

The Wonders of the Lord
(A Prayer of Worship)

Key Thought: The wonders of the Lord lead us into the wonderful realm of worship.

Key Scripture: *"Many, O Lord my God, are Your wonderful works which You have done; And Your thoughts toward us Cannot be recounted to You in order; if I would declare and speak of them, They are more than can be numbered"* *(Ps. 40:5, NKJV).*

Prayer: When I meditate upon your wondrous works, O Lord, I am reminded of your majesty, your splendor, and your mighty power. Thank you for revealing your wonders to me through your Word and your moving in my life.

You caused the sun to stand still and the moon to stay put so that your people could take vengeance upon their enemies.[1] You divided the Red Sea so that your people could enter the Promised Land.[2] You sent manna to be their food.[3] You healed multitudes of people.[4] You have promised so many things to your family.[5] I praise you and adore you, Father.

Many, O Lord, are your wonderful works.[6] Your works in my life are marvelous in my eyes,[7] and they are a witness to those who do not know you. I stand amazed in your presence, and when I look upon the world you have made, I am awed by your mighty power, your creativity, and your love. The way of an eagle in the air, the way of a serpent upon a rock, the way of a ship in the midst of the sea, and the way of a man with a maid are all wonders of your creation.[8] You have created all things for your pleasure, Lord, and I want to bring pleasure to you as well.[9]

You have promised to work such a work in our midst that we will not be able to believe or comprehend it even though someone tells us about it.[10] Thank you for this promise and for the certain knowledge that you are able to do exceeding abundantly above all that I can ask or think.[11] The heavens declare your glory, Lord, and the firmament shows forth your handiwork.[12] Those who behold your perfect creation are without excuse.[13]

It thrills me to realize that eye has not seen, nor ear heard, neither has it entered into the human heart, all the things which you have prepared for those who love you.[14] Thank you, Father. You alone are worthy to receive honor, glory, and power, for you have created all things.[15]

References: *(1) Joshua 10:13; (2) Psalms 106:9; (3) Psalms 78:24; (4) Mark 1:34; (5) 2 Peter 1:4; (6) Psalms 40:5; (7) Psalms 118:23; (8) Proverbs 30:19; (9) Revelation 4:11; (10) Habakkuk 1:5; (11) Ephesians 3:20; (12) Psalms 19:1; (13) Romans 1:20; (14) 1 Corinthians 2:9; (15) Revelation 4:11.*

MORE PRAYERS THAT PREVAIL

Prayer Journal

Date	Notes and Comments

Date	Notes and Comments

Prayer Journal

Date	Notes and Comments

Date	Notes and Comments

Date	Notes and Comments

Date	Notes and Comments

Date	Notes and Comments

Date	Notes and Comments

Date	Notes and Comments

Date	Notes and Comments

Date	Notes and Comments

Date	Notes and Comments

PRAYER CLASSIC

Pray God's Word - Receive His Promises

Praying God's Word puts His dynamic power to work and energizes your faith. *Prayers That Prevail* is a practical manual for building an effective prayer life. This essential tool is filled with prayers and scriptures that address more than 100 topics of vital concern to every believer.

MORE PRAYERS THAT PREVAIL

Praying in the Will of God

"...if we ask anything according to his will, he hears us..." (1 John 5:14, NIV). God's will is revealed in His Word. When we pray His Word, therefore, we can be confident that we are praying His will. This is the foundational truth on which the ever-popular *Prayers That Prevail* series has been built.

More Prayers That Prevail equips the believer with tremendous resources for dynamic prayer that will prevail in every area of life:

- More topical prayers related to personal concerns
- More keys to answered prayer
- More principles of prayer from the Word
- More thoughts on prayer from prayer warriors
- More faith-building testimonies of prevailing prayer
- More prayer promises from the Bible

PRAYERS FOR AMERICA

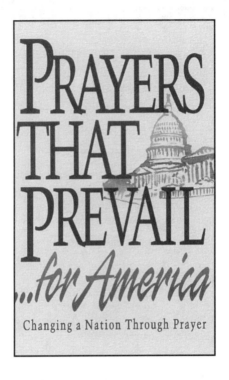

PRAYERS THAT PREVAIL FOR AMERICA – Changing a Nation Through Prayer: An Intercessor's Manual by the authors of the best-selling *Prayers That Prevail.* Learn how to pray God's powerful promises in behalf of our nation, our leaders, our people and our problems. Take America back through sixty topical prayers from the Bible that invoke God's blessings and mercy for our land. In addition to the prayers, this dynamic book includes "A Call to Intercession," a look at "The Presidents and Prayer," "One Nation Under God," and "Fifty Prayer Promises." For every Christian who is concerned about America.

AVAILABLE AT YOUR CHRISTIAN BOOKSTORE
OR FROM
VICTORY HOUSE
(See order form in back of book)

PRAYERS FOR CHILDREN AND GRANDCHILDREN

Prayers That Prevail for Your Children

When Believing parents pray God's promises for their children or grandchildren, amazing things always happen. God hears and answers the prayers of godly parents. He protects the children, guides them, strengthens them and blesses them. God's wisdom is imparted to the parent, and the parent-child relationship is solidified.

Prayers That Prevail for Your Children is a treasured resource for every parent and grandparent. Unique on today's market, this book provides parents and grandparents with a now perspective on their important ministry to their children and grandchildren – a dynamic partnership with God.

AVAILABLE AT YOUR CHRISTIAN BOOKSTORE
OR FROM VICTORY HOUSE
(See order form in back of book)

– GIFT BOOKS –

FOR WOMEN

Brighten your day with the diamonds of truth, pearls of wisdom, and gems of joy that sparkle on every page of this inspiring book. Its uplifting and thought-provoking words will keep you going, laughing, learning, and loving on even the most trying days.

Written by women for women, *A Little Bit of God's Wisdom & Wit for Women* is the perfect gift for that special friend or even for yourself. This little book is one that Women everywhere will cherish and enjoy for years to come.

FOR THE MEN TOO

This handy book has been designed by men for men. Wisdom from the Bible and witty sayings from the pens of men will give the readers insights into life and success. Small enough to be taken anywhere, a man will enjoy reading this book wherever he may go, providing relief from tension, truths to take hold of, and humor to brighten his day.

AVAILABLE AT YOUR CHRISTIAN BOOKSTORE
OR FROM VICTORY HOUSE
(See order form in back of book)

– GIFT BOOKS –

FOR EVERYONE

A Little Bit of God's Wisdom & Wit

You will laugh, feel challenged, learn new truths, and desire to become the best you can be as you take just a few moments to glean fresh insights into God's wisdom and the witty sayings of men and women, past and present.

An ideal giftbook for all occasions, *A Little Bit of God's Wisdom and Wit* will find its way into the hearts, homes and hands of people everywhere.

AVAILABLE AT YOUR CHRISTIAN BOOKSTORE
OR FROM
VICTORY HOUSE
(See order form in back of book)

Prayer Requests

Your prayer needs are important to us.
If you have a prayer request — just write to
Clift Richards & Lloyd Hildebrand at:

Victory House, Inc.
"Prayers That Prevail"
P.O. Box 700238
Tulsa, OK 74170

BOOK ORDER FORM

To order additional books by Clift Richards and Lloyd Hildebrand direct from the publisher, please use this order form. Also note that your local bookstore can order titles for you.

Book Title	Price	Qty.	Amount
Prayers That Prevail	$9.99	_____	$_____
More Prayers That Prevail	$8.99	_____	$_____
Prayers That Prevail for America	$9.99	_____	$_____
Prayers That Prevail for Your Children	$9.99	_____	$_____
A Little Bit of God's Wisdom & Wit	$5.99	_____	$_____
A Little Bit of God's Wisdom & Wit for Men	$5.99	_____	$_____
A Little Bit of God's Wisdom & Wit for Women	$5.99	_____	$_____

Total Book Amount	$_____
Shipping & Handling — Add $2.00 for the **first** book, **plus** $0.50 for **each** additional book.	$_____
TOTAL ORDER AMOUNT — *Enclose check or money order. (No cash or C.O.D.'s.)*	$_____

Make check or money order payable to: **VICTORY HOUSE, INC.**

Mail order to: **Victory House, Inc.**
                        P.O Box 700238
                        Tulsa, OK 74170

Please print your name and address **clearly:**

Name _____

Address _____

City _____

State or Province _____

Zip or Postal Code _____

Telephone Number (_____) _____

Foreign orders must be submittted in U.S. dollars. Foreign orders are shipped by uninsured surface mail. We ship all orders within 48 hours of receipt of order.

MasterCard or VISA — For credit card orders you may use your MasterCard or VISA by completing the following information, or for **faster service,** call toll-free **1-800-262-2631**.

Card Name _____

Card Number _____

Expiration Date _____

Signature _____
                   (authorized signature)

BOOK ORDER FORM

To order additional books by Clift Richards and Lloyd Hildebrand direct from the publisher, please use this order form. Also note that your local bookstore can order titles for you.

Book Title	Price	Qty.	Amount
Prayers That Prevail	$9.99	_____	$_____
More Prayers That Prevail	$8.99	_____	$_____
Prayers That Prevail for America	$9.99	_____	$_____
Prayers That Prevail for Your Children	$9.99	_____	$_____
A Little Bit of God's Wisdom & Wit	$5.99	_____	$_____
A Little Bit of God's Wisdom & Wit for Men	$5.99	_____	$_____
A Little Bit of God's Wisdom & Wit for Women	$5.99	_____	$_____

Total Book Amount $_____

*Shipping & Handling — Add $2.00 for the **first** book, **plus** $0.50 for **each** additional book.* $_____

TOTAL ORDER AMOUNT *— Enclose check or money order. (No cash or C.O.D.'s.)* $_____

Make check or money order payable to: **VICTORY HOUSE, INC.**

Mail order to: **Victory House, Inc.
P.O Box 700238
Tulsa, OK 74170**

Please print your name and address **clearly:**

Name _____

Address _____

City _____

State or Province _____

Zip or Postal Code _____

Telephone Number (_____) _____

Foreign orders must be submittted in U.S. dollars. Foreign orders are shipped by uninsured surface mail. We ship all orders within 48 hours of receipt of order.

MasterCard or VISA — For credit card orders you may use your MasterCard or VISA by completing the following information, or for **faster service,** call toll-free **1-800-262-2631**.

Card Name _____

Card Number _____

Expiration Date _____

Signature _____
(authorized signature)